# Animals Don't Know There Exists A Tomorrow

# OrangeBooks Publication

1st Floor, Rajhans Arcade, Mall Road, Kohka, Bhilai, Chhattisgarh 490020

Website: **www.orangebooks.in**

**First Edition, 2024**

**ISBN:** 978-93-6554-458-9

**Price:** Rs. 399.00

The opinions/ contents expressed in this book are solely of the author and do not represent the opinions/ standings/ thoughts of OrangeBooks.

Printed in India

# MONASTERIES IN THE WILD

## nags

Sai Niranjan Nagu

**OrangeBooks Publication**
www.orangebooks.in

# About the Author

The author, an IT professional with over three decades of experience working with clients worldwide, spent five years in his youth living in an ashram in India. Drawing from this wealth of experience in work and life, he has distilled his insights into a book inspired by the animal kingdom. Through the simple question, 'If an animal can, can't we?' the book invites readers to explore the valuable lessons animals have to offer.

As you journey through the pages (the jungle), you'll discover a wealth of lessons from these humble beings, even though they possess no formal degrees and do not boast of their knowledge.

The author's journey into the world of animals began with the arrival of his beloved child Veera (his pet dog), on March 14, 2012. From that moment, a magical journey unfolded. Gazing into Veera's eyes, he realized that if there was so much to learn from just one animal, there must be countless lessons to learn from the vast array of creatures in the jungle. Thus, he embarked on this enlightening journey.

Whether by coincidence or driven by an innate desire, he encountered animals in every part of his ventures outside of work. As he delved deeper into the wonders of the animal kingdom, he discovered that it wasn't just about the animals themselves; rather, there existed a 'jungle of gurus' in the wilderness, offering life lessons, ideologies, inventions, love, corporate insights, and family values. Each aspect of the jungle held its own treasures, waiting to be unearthed and explored.

The author shares his experiences with the animal kingdom in this book, offering the lessons he has learned from these humble beings over time. Join him as we embark on a journey into the heart of the wilderness.

❧

**This book is a copy right of BaraEmpneo (BE)**

We encourage readers to extract information from this book for educational purposes that may benefit them and their audience. Our aim is to share knowledge and insights that can contribute to personal and professional growth. Feel free to utilize the content in a manner that enriches your understanding and facilitates learning.

**Disclaimer:** This book draws inspiration from a beloved pet. In an earnest quest to explore the animal kingdom, the author extensively researched information from various sources, including the internet and literature about animals worldwide.

The core ideology of this book is to share the wealth of knowledge acquired from the animal kingdom, aligning it with teachings relevant to both the corporate world and personal life. It is hoped that readers will find value in these insights, enabling them to lead happier and more fulfilling lives, both in the workplace and in their personal spheres.

# Dedication

---◄◇►---

To my beloved child

*"Veera"*

14th Mar 2012 – 06th May 2023

4070 days of love

***"Nothing But Love"***

*It was through his eyes,*

*that I was introduced to the fascinating world of animals.*

**"An Eye Opener"**

❧

# Gratitude

To Veera, the angel.

*"எங்கிருந்தோ வந்தான் இடைச்சாதி நான் என்றான்*

*இங்கிவனை யான் பெறவே என்ன தவம் செய்து விட்டேன்"*

**"Where did he come from, what great penance have I
done to have had him in my life"
SubramanyaBharathi**

*Writer, Poet & Freedom fighter (1882 – 1921)*

"Thank you" may be too simple a phrase in the English
language, yet it is the only means I have, to convey my
profound gratitude to this wonderful angel, my beloved
pet Veera, who decorated twelve years of my life with his
presence.

I didn't just fall in love with him, or with the breed, or
even with dogs or pets in general. I fell in love with the
entire world of animals. It was he who opened my eyes to
behold the beauty of this wondrous world. It was he who
made me understand that there exists a world where love,
and only love, permeates every nook and corner, in all
four directions, North, South, East, and West. In all four
seasons, Summer, Winter, Spring, and Autumn. It
saturates every square inch of their world, every sight they
behold, every breath they take, and every move they

make. In their world, it is "Nothing but Love" and love alone.

Can someone get 101 out of 100 in an exam? A BIG NO is our answer – right?

But, in my view, pets are the ones who can love you.

*"366 out of 365 Days in a year*

*13 out of 12 Months in a year*

*8 out of 7 Days in a week*

*25 out of 24 Hours in a day*

*61 out of 60 Minutes in an hour*

*61 out of 60 Seconds in a Minute"*

If you want to understand the true meaning of the word "unconditional love," do not search for it in the dictionary, for no language in the world can articulate it better than pets. They alone have the power to demonstrate the essence of unconditional love. Just as writing or holding a picture of fire isn't enough to feel its heat, you must stand next to it to experience it. My humble advice to the readers is: "This life is only once; do not miss the chance to experience the love of an animal."

There are countless videos on YouTube with titles like "Top 3 Things to Do Before You Die" or "Top 3 Places to Visit Before You Die." However, in my opinion, experiencing the love of a pet should undoubtedly be one of the top three things on your bucket list before you kick the bucket.

It's undeniable that dogs serve as stressbusters and provide invaluable support with disorders like autism or ADHD, guiding the blind, and so on. However, beyond their therapeutic roles, there are numerous life lessons to learn from them. They teach us how to find happiness, maintain peace, live in the present moment, share, care, and above all, love unconditionally. My inspiration to write this book stemmed from my beloved pet, who motivated me to spread the message that the jungle is home to countless wonderful beings, each with valuable teachings for mankind. This book is my humble offering to honor this beautiful angel who decorated my life.

A short note on Veera on the day he left us:

> *"Who loves amma (mother) the most at home,*
> *it was Veera!*
>
> *Who loves appa (father) the most at home,*
> *it was Veera!*
>
> *Who loves Sai Anna (brother) the most at home,*
> *it was Veera!*
>
> *Who loves Sathya Anna (brother) the most at home,*
> *it was Veera!*
>
> *There was no one else, who could love us*
> *more than him!"*

Such is the love pets show us. Some people make this world a beautiful place just by living in it, and Veera was one of those. I dedicate this book and my time to this wonderful being.

> *"Thank you, Veera"*

My heartfelt thanks go out to the individuals who played a pivotal role in inspiring and supporting me throughout this journey. They were the keys to unlocking the door to this magnificent world.

## To my wife Navaneeth

For a long time, both my sons had been pestering us to get a pet at home. However, our response was always a resounding "NO," like that of most other parents. The list of justifications for saying no was much longer than that for saying yes, which was more than enough to convince them to deny their plea. Having a dog at home is a responsibility because from day one until its last day, it's like having a child at home. One fine day, my wife asked, "How about gifting a pet for Sai's (my elder son's) birthday?" In our house, everything revolves around the lady at home, and thus, on the 14th of March 2012, a 45-day-old puppy, a new furry family member, arrived. My wife named him "Veera." Thanks to my wife, Navaneeth, if not for her decision, I would not have ventured into the jungle.

## My son's Sai & Sathya

As parents, we all strive to fulfill the desires of our children. I am fortunate to have two children who harbored this wonderful desire. It was for them that we changed our lifestyle, and the lessons we learned along the way were invaluable life lessons. It was all because of them. At times, children teach great lessons to parents, we realized this late, but better late than never.

**To my friends Kishore and Amba**

Thanks to this wonderful couple who introduced us to the world of animals. It was by seeing their pet dog, Tango, that my sons were inspired to have a pet at home. Their house has been a home to many animals, including tortoises and snakes, during floods and COVID times.

I still vividly recall the thank-you note I wrote to this couple on the day Veera passed away. Despite the sorrow that engulfed us, it was also a moment to convey our gratitude. If not for them, we might never have experienced this greater love.

**Thanks to Hubra Digital**

We would like to express our sincere appreciation to Kishore and the esteemed team at Hubra Digital. Your exceptional skill and commitment have significantly enhanced our project, culminating in a cover that beautifully reflects the essence of our work.

**Special Thanks to the man behind the scenes**

A heartfelt thanks to my son, Sai Niranjan, who played the key role in bringing this book to completion. He has been my first critic and my first supporter, serving as a mentor at times despite his younger age, and always motivating me to push forward. He's been an idea generator, a source of encouragement, and much more. Our late-night conversations, often stretching into the early hours, were filled with discussions about our work. Without his unwavering support and insight, this book would not have been possible.

**- Be Happy Always -**

❧

# Foreword

When I was asked to write a foreword for "Monasteries in the wild", I felt both honored and excited. This book offers a refreshing perspective on life, drawing from the profound lessons we can learn from animals—a perspective that is often overlooked in our fast-paced, goal- oriented world.

It all began with my mentor's bond with his pet dog, Veera, whom I first met when he was just 2 years old in 2014. I still remember talking about Veera to my wife—how his unconditional love sparked a curiosity in my mentor: If there is so much to learn from one animal, what other lessons might nature have to offer? From this initial inspiration, he embarked on a journey that led him to encounters with elephants, birds, bees, pandas, and whales—each with a story to tell and, most importantly, lessons that we can learn from their way of living.

What resonates with me most about this book is its simple yet profound message: aim to be happy rather than just successful. This idea is beautifully illustrated through the carefree life of pandas—"eat, sleep, play, repeat"—reminding us that joy can be found in the simplest routines. Similarly, the well-organized elephant herds offer insights into leadership, community, and empathy—qualities that are vital not just in the animal kingdom, but in our own lives and organizations as well.

I was particularly struck by the fascinating concept of the 'V' formation of birds—a symbol of unity, strength, and the seamless transfer of knowledge across generations. It reminded me of one of my own philosophies: "If you want to live long, you can live through generations only by transferring your knowledge." This aligns with my core belief that knowledge, when shared, becomes a legacy that endures beyond any single lifetime.

The section on bees is equally captivating. These industrious creatures, with their remarkable work ethic and complex communication systems, show us what it means to contribute selflessly to a greater cause. Their tireless efforts to sustain the green world around us are a testament to dedication and the power of community.

And then there are the whales, whose friendly nature and ability to teach one another highlight the importance of compassion and mentorship. Their behavior serves as a gentle reminder that the greatest leaders are often the most humble and the most generous with their wisdom.

But perhaps the most profound question posed by this book is: "If birds can, why can't we? If bees can, why can't we? If elephants can, why can't we? If pandas can, why can't we? If whales can, why can't we?" If animals can inherently understand the importance of community, leadership, work ethics, cooperation, happiness, and knowledge-sharing, what stops us, as humans, from doing the same?

"Monasteries in the wild" invites us to open our eyes to the wisdom all around us, to learn from the world in its purest form, and to embrace love as a guiding principle in all that we do. I hope you find these pages as enlightening and inspiring as I did. May they encourage you to reflect, grow, and most importantly, to love without conditions.

With deep respect and admiration,

**Prakash Palani**

**Founder & CTO of Basis Cloud Solutions (BCS)**

# Contents

# The Why?

**Why write this book?**

**"There is no greater agony
than bearing an untold story inside you"**

**Maya Angelou**

I t's not merely the pain of leaving a story untold; it's the yearning to spread the message that I have learnt over many years, that there are countless lessons to be learned from the vast expanse of teachers in the jungle that would help us in our day to day life style as well as in our office space, there are great life lessons, there are a jungle of Gurus in the jungle. Inspiration surrounds us every day, from dawn to dusk and beyond, all twenty-four hours a day, it is for us to keep our eyes and ears open. Like it is said,

*"God is always talking to us, it is we who do not listen"*

Similar is the story of the day-to-day city dwellers, many, or most of us have not looked into the forests for inspiration, we always feel that the forests are for the animals or for the renunciant and not for the common man. This book is an attempt to reboot professional and personal spaces, offering fresh perspective and new learnings from the forests.

Not many in this world get to experience this greater living, to experience the companionship of an animal in their lifetime, though it is the easiest. We always strive for the hardest, missing to notice the easiest ones that are just next to us. I was gifted to have an experience with an animal, as I looked into his eyes, something struck deep in my heart and mind, that there must be a wealth of knowledge waiting to be discovered from other animals as well. And so, the magical journey began, continuing until this very day. I am certain it will persist until the last day of my life, for I firmly and always believed that "it is

the journey that is more beautiful than the destination".
Time may fade like the wind, but memories endure.

"யான் பெற்ற இன்பம் பெறுக இவ்வையகம்"
- திரு மந்திரம்

**"Let thy experience the bliss I have gained"
- Thirumandiram**

Every journey begins with the first step. Mine was taken
on the 14th of March 2012. Initially, I embarked on this
journey as a mere traveler. However, as I delved deeper
into the forests, day by day, I came to realize that another
beautiful world exists within our own. I believe that
heaven and hell are not distant realms up above in the sky;
rather, they reside right where we live. It is up to us to
decide whether it's heaven or hell, for it is our hearts and
minds that must make the choice.

There was a lesson in every step I took into the forests, in
every page I read, in every word I heard, for every
situation in life. Just as we turn to the Bhagavad Gita or
the bible for solutions during times of trouble and find
answers, so too do these wonderful creatures offer
solutions to every problem and countless lessons for every
walk of life.

In this journey, I realized that there are many lessons for
corporate goers. Throughout my 35- year career as an IT
professional, I have undergone and conducted numerous
corporate trainings on soft skills and many other technical
areas. These skills are essential for corporate success. I
was surprised that we, as six-sensed beings, had to

3

undergo training in colleges and again in corporates on these fronts, whereas animals seem to possess these techniques instinctively, without language skills, university degrees, or certifications.

Compared to years past, today we hear more about health issues and the loss of life among youngsters. When I was young, hearing about someone's death usually meant they were old, typically above 60 years of age. But now, we increasingly hear about young people dying from health issues like heart attacks or cancer, often due to poor eating habits, lack of exercise, work-life imbalance, and work-related stress. Pollution further adds to these problems, adding fuel to the fire. The very reason for this situation is that we have picked up very well on the technical skills and missed out on the life management skills, it is like venturing into the sea alone in a motorboat not knowing swimming and with no life jacket. This book is an attempt to equip oneself on life skills apart from technical skills and career growth.

*"Aim not for the moon or the stars, but for happiness! It is more important to be happy at the end of the day, Whether you are in moon, star or the earth!"*

*- BE*

There are lessons not just for corporate professionals, but also for environmentalists, students, and families on living cohesively, raising children, passing on values, and much more.

Moreover, the jungle offers numerous life lessons: how to find consistent happiness, how to live for today rather than tomorrow, and many others. I was surprised to

4

discover that some animals provide services worth billions of dollars, free of cost—services that corporations would charge heavily for. We will explore more of these insights together on this journey into the jungle.

I have been lucky that I had an encounter with an animal in every journey I made out of my routine work, through this journey, I discovered many of life's values and decided to compile them so that readers may benefit from them.

## The journey from "Nothing but Love" to "Monasteries in the wild"

The greatest message from this furry messenger was simply this: 'Love, Nothing But Love.' The messenger is gone, but his message endures. In his eyes, I saw the door of a monastery open wide, inviting me on a journey from 'nothing but love' to the sacred wilderness, where the heart finds its own monastery in the wild. Thus, the transition from "Nothing But Love" to "Monasteries in the wild".

If the extract of this book is about the "how-to" of life, how to be happy, how to socialize, how to succeed in corporate and personal life, how to build a team, how to be a good team player, how to improve on communication, how to adapt to changes, how to be a good mentor or mentee, how to deal with clients, how to negotiate, how to achieve work-life balance, how to navigate through challenges, even in the face of adversity, etc - you may be puzzled about the relevance of love in this context, aren't you?

The answer lies in realizing that through love, one can understand these concepts by observing the animal kingdom in a simpler way. Not only faith, but love can also move mountains.

In corporate trainings, the typical references often include the top and successful personalities such as Bill Gates, Steve Jobs, and others of similar cadre. There is no doubt that these figures are truly inspiring, but achieving their level of success is not easy. You can pose a question: "If Bill Gates can, can´t you?", the answer is a definite yes, but only one in a million reaches such heights, and it is not without an immense amount of hard work behind the scenes. In this journey, we will explore what a small bird is capable of, posing the simple question "if a bird can, can't we?". If you have doubts, try building a nest and placing it securely in a tree. You'll understand the difficulty even though you have two hands to help, while a small bird builds it without hands. Their forests and grasslands are boundless realms of learning.

**Why call it "unconditional love"?**

"Take any relationship, whether it's between husband and wife, father and son, mother and daughter, brother and sister, or teacher and student; conflicts are unavoidable. Differences of opinion and moments of bitterness are bound to arise. This love often comes with conditions; it fluctuates depending on the smoothness of the relationship. If everything is going well, the love may be at 100%, but you will see a drop in the % when faced with challenges. It isn´t the case with animals. Their love is unwavering. They offer their affection consistently, regardless of circumstances. Their only requirement is your presence; simply being with them is enough to make them happy.

There's a joke that goes like this: Imagine you accidentally lock your spouse in a room when leaving to office in the morning, and when you return home in the evening, just imagine the state of the house. But if you purposely lock your pet and return in the evening, you'll see the difference. Rather than being upset about being locked in the whole day, your pet will be overjoyed that you've come back to see him again.

*"If there is a book you really want to read but it hasn't been written yet, then you must write it"*

**Toni Morrison**

*- Be Happy Always*

♣

# *The What?*

**What is there to learn from the jungle?**

## Common sense

We humans proudly consider ourselves as having a sixth sense, believing it places us above beings with one to five senses. Trees and plants are often considered to have one sense, snails and corals two senses, ants and worms three senses, crabs and beetles four senses, and birds and animals five senses. The seventh sense, however, remains something beyond the reach of the human mind.

When faced with life's challenges, we often turn to our own intellect for guidance. Yet, profound teachings can be found among beings with senses less developed than ours. How these creatures acquire and transmit their knowledge across generations, without language, writing, or computer, remains a mystery beyond our understanding. While humans rely on language for communication, the ability of animals to convey and preserve values without words is a fascinating mystery. This book seeks to draw inspiration from the wisdom of the jungle, focusing not on the origins of these insights, but on their potential to enrich our lives.

## The simple logic of being happy.

*"Animals do not know there exists a tomorrow,*

*So, they live for today" – BE*

Conversely, humans, burdened with the knowledge of mortality and the uncertainty of tomorrow´s arrival, often dwell on the future and overlook the joys of today. This was particularly evident during the Covid pandemic, where people rushed to stockpile essentials, worrying more about tomorrow's scarcity. The comical part is, I

9

heard from a friend of mine in the US that the first shelf to get emptied were the toilet papers, why stock toilet paper when you are doubtful about the availability of intake?

And animals do not expect support from their offspring in old age; they rely solely on their own capacities. In contrast, humans often plan for the future, to have children so that they may have someone to care for them in their old age or to save for their children. This attitude reflects our tendency to sacrifice the present for the sake of tomorrow, a trait absent in the animal kingdom, where living for today takes precedence.

A guru isn't confined to the image of a person in a saffron robe, meditating under a tree or preaching. They can manifest in anyone around us, permeating every corner of the cosmos, ready to offer guidance when needed. It's up to us to attune ourselves to their frequency and seek solutions to our problems. This endeavor aims to awaken the seeker within us to find wisdom from the teachers of the jungle.

*"Buddham saranam gachami*

*Dhammam saranam gachami*

*Sangam saranam gachami"*


*"Take refuge at the feet of an evolved soul!*

*The teacher may leave, but his teachings live!*

*Surround yourself with the right-minded people!"*.

It's true that the Buddha, the Enlightened One, shared countless life lessons while sitting under a tree in a forest. This book is an attempt to show that there are many Buddhas around trees deep inside the forest, and to discover the lessons they have to offer us.

## Animals and Religion

Animals have long been intertwined with religious beliefs across cultures. In both the Bible and the Quran, there are mentions of animals, such as the donkey, symbolizing different aspects. Hinduism, one of the oldest religions, fully incorporates animals into its beliefs. Many animals are associated with specific gods or goddesses, such as the bull and snake with Shiva, the eagle with Vishnu, and swan with Brahma and so on.

In my perspective, attaching animals as carriers for gods, known as vahana, served a purpose in ancient times. By instilling fear of the gods in people's minds, certain norms and values were upheld in society. Recognizing that the world is created for all creatures, not just humans, each animal may have been associated with a deity to ensure their protection. By fearing the gods, people were encouraged to refrain from causing harm to the animals associated with them.

In today's world, there is a growing realization of the importance of conserving both animals and forests. Strict laws are being enforced to protect these vital ecosystems, ensuring the coexistence of humans and animals on the same planet. It's widely understood that this world is not solely for humans; animals deserve their rightful space and respect. Moreover, scientists are actively researching alternatives to traditional meat consumption, recognizing the environmental impact of livestock farming. These efforts signify a shift towards more sustainable practices that benefit both humans and the natural world.

I once saw a banner with animals, led by a chimpanzee holding a board that read 'It's our world too.' It created a lot of questions within me about whether what we as humans were doing to the animals was right or not. Not only to the animals but to this whole world; in turn, we are creating all this chaos for ourselves. The future of mankind doesn't really sound very kind. I once heard someone say, if there were no humans in this world, with only animals on all continents, it would flourish with no pollution of any sort, which is very true because they take only what they need for the day. But we take for tomorrow and the day after as well, not only for ourselves but for the next two generations too.

In this book, we will take a walk into the forest, examining each animal and endeavoring to understand what it has to teach humans about our day-to-day lifestyle and corporate life, as well as the life lessons these animals impart. Are we only going to focus on the lessons to be learned? No, there is much more. We will also explore some of the very strange facts that revolve around each of these animals. Like,

➤ Can males get pregnant?

➤ Can any animal exist with no heart and no brain?

➤ What could be the maximum weight of a bird's nest?

> Will you drink a beer that is made out of the poop?

> For some, purpose of life is just to mate and then die.

> Some of the animals that currently reside solely in the sea were once land animals.

> The attraction between opposite sexes is common across the planet, not just among humans, but also in plants, which survive by mating. Did you know there is a species that shows no interest in mating at all, yet has persisted for millions of years?

> How do you resolve fights and conflicts – through a police station or a court – right? Can you resolve conflicts just by love? Yes, you can.

> Can you imagine some beings having two stomachs? Sounds weird, isn´t it?

Did you immediately wonder "how could that be?", while reading these lines before consulting Mr. Google?

Can males get pregnant?

Yes, nature has its own way of working, male seahorses and sea dragons get pregnant and bear young, a unique adaptation in the animal kingdom.

Can any animal exist with no heart and no brain?

Jellyfish is an aquatic animal that does not contain a brain, heart, or lungs. There are others in the ocean with similar traits.

Read on for more intriguing, strange, and fun facts.

At times, some of us compare humans to animals as a means of denigration. Yet, upon closer examination of our value systems, it becomes evident that we should be the ones feeling ashamed for making such comparisons. Consider this simple logic: everything emitted by a human, be it excretion, spit, sweat, or anything else, carries a foul odor. The only exception seems to be words. However, do we always ensure that our words are uplifting and beneficial is a question. Furthermore, even after death, the human body serves no purpose; it must be either cremated or buried as soon as possible.

Consider the case of animals: a whale is worth a fortune while alive, and once deceased, still does lot of good for other oceanic creatures. Many parts of an elephant hold immense value, from its tusks in the front to its dung at the back. Even the excrement of a cow possesses antimicrobial and antioxidant properties. Biogas also known as Gobar Gas is produced through the anaerobic decomposition of organic wastes from animals and plants. Whale vomit is utilized in the production of perfumes, and whale feces holds significant value. Therefore, comparing humans to animals is like comparing apples to lemons.

### Do you know which is the most dangerous animal in this world?

The African continent boasts dense forests teeming with wildlife, including some of the most dangerous predators on the planet. It's a land abundant in natural resources, where the fertility of the soil is so remarkable that seeds can sprout effortlessly without any additional care. This close connection to nature and wildlife is evident throughout the region.

Survival in this environment has always been about adaptation and resilience; those who can't adapt risk extinction. We're witnessing many species facing extinction, and it's not inconceivable that future generations might only read about today's lions and tigers in history books, much like we do with dinosaurs. While the dinosaurs were wiped out by a meteoroid, today's animals face extinction due to human activities.

Humans are highly adaptable creatures, often likened to chameleons for their ability to change rapidly. However, our rapid population growth is putting immense pressure on resources, leading to habitat loss and deforestation, which in turn threatens animal populations. This loss of habitat and biodiversity is primarily driven by human greed rather than genuine need.

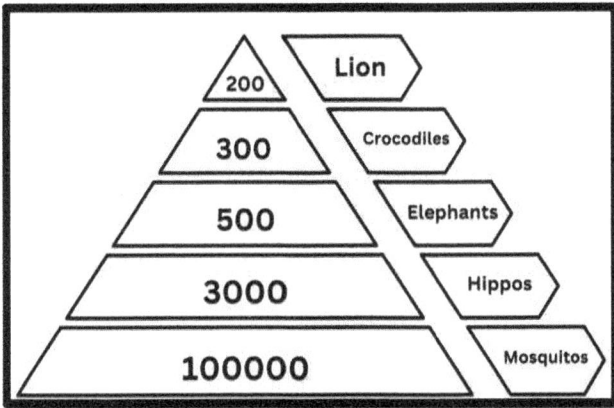

From this analysis, we discover that the most dangerous animal is not the King of the jungle, the Lion, nor the formidable predator, the Crocodile, nor even the largest, the Elephant, or the heaviest, the Hippo. Surprisingly, it is the mosquito, weighing just 2.5 grams, that holds the title of the most dangerous creature of all.

Note: Humans are not included in the above analysis, as they would undoubtedly top the list otherwise. Consider the number of deaths caused by humans through warfare throughout history. We are among the few species that engage in killing our own kind, often discriminating based on color, creed and greed for land and power.

Their life is their message, they communicate not with languages of the mouth but with the language of the heart. By listening to them, we can understand and gain insights.

Sit back, relax, and enjoy your journey. I'll be your pilot today as we venture into the forest, step by step. Along the way, I'll provide insights into each animal we encounter, offering lessons to learn from their way of living, as well as sharing strange and fun facts about their lifestyle.

Let's take a walk alongside the four-legged monks to the "Monasteries in the Wild".

*"There is something to learn in everything" – BE*

*- Be Happy Always –*

🌿

# The Gentle Giants

**"This earth was made for all being, not just human beings"**

L et us begin our journey in India, where tradition dictates seeking the blessings of the revered elephant god, Ganesha, before embarking on any auspicious endeavor. As we take our first step into the jungle, where mighty herds of elephants' roam, we are reminded of the profound connection between humanity and these gentle giants. In my view, observing an elephant is a form of meditation. There may be different forms of meditation and various interpretations, whatever be the method, the end result expected out of meditation is to be at peace. The core of meditation lies in cultivating a serene and contented mind. Watching the grace of an elephant can effortlessly induce this state, is my humble view.

To get a real feel of this truth, pay a visit to a temple or a zoo, sit just a little away from the elephant, watch every graceful movement of this gentle giant and you will find that in its presence, a sense of peace washes over you, and you will be drenched with tranquility long after you depart. Whether it is a playful calf or a wise elderly one, it does not matter; its innocence, irrespective of its age, will awaken the child within you, that we often neglect. Observing elephants is a true blessing. In the midst of this busy life, as we run around in search of something, it is often the smallest pleasures that bring us the greatest joy. This principle is like the timeless wisdom of the 80/20 rule, where it's those 20% of little things that give us 80% of immense joy. Indeed, elephants are not just revered in India but in lands far and wide, embodying a universal symbol of reverence and awe.

Before we start to take a walk along the herd path in the forests, let's take a moment to delve a little into the spiritual realm. Initially, a stone is merely a piece of rock, but with the skill of a sculptor, it transforms. When crafted into the likeness of Ganesha, we believe it holds the power to remove obstacles from our lives. Similarly, a statue of Lord Venkateshwara is believed to bring wealth, while one of Buddha symbolizes peace and harmony. Thus, it's not the stone itself, but the faith it embodies that imparts these varied benefits, it is your thoughts, it is your belief that makes the magic happen. How else could the same stone, assuming different forms, offer such diverse blessings? In the words of tamil poet Kannadasan,

கண்ணிலே அன்பிருந்தால் கல்லிலே
தெய்வம் வரும்

**"You can find God in the stone, if there is
love in the eyes."**

**In search of elephants, in Sri Lanka** – The journey to Sri Lanka felt like stepping into a paradise of lush greenery and warm-hearted hospitality. It was an adventurous journey with a vibrant flow of experiences, from calm beaches and foggy hill stations to sacred pilgrimage sites like Ashoka Vanam from the Ramayana and the revered Temple of the Tooth Relic, a Buddhist temple in Kandy that houses the Buddha's tooth relic. While there was a unique charm in every stop, it was our stay in a village near Udawalawe, famous for its elephant sanctuary, that truly captured our hearts. More than a pilgrimage or an adventure trip, it ended up being an educational voyage for me.

Our voyage began in Colombo, winding its way to the quaint hill station of Nuwara Eliya, nestled in central Sri Lanka. Along the way, my friend suggested a detour to Pinnawala Elephant orphanage, to witness the grand elephant parade. However, the term seemed distressing to hear, I would have been happy if it was called an elephant sanctuary than an orphanage.

We immersed ourselves in watching the elephants being nurtured and cared for. Elephant feeding was something that I witnessed for the first time. Tourists were given long cans of milk with which they could feed them. The eagerness to witness the grand parade was building steadily, and the wait was richly rewarded when a magnificent procession unfolded before our eyes. Through the bustling market street lined with shops on both sides and full of people, they marched their way to the Maha Oya River, a few hundred meters away, to take a dip. It was a visual treat to watch these adorable giants of various sizes march towards the river for a bath. It would be more apt to call it "playtime" similar to the PT period we used to have during school days, which we all eagerly awaited. Here, it was a similar experience not only for the elephants but also for the people watching. People standing nearby were occasionally drenched by splashes of water as the elephants used their trunks to cool themselves.

Later, on my return, a search in google revealed a varied view of the orphanage, on the way these majestic creatures were treated, some suggested not to visit this place as these lovable creatures were treated like prisoners. Like there are two sides to a coin, it is quite natural to have varied views. But I talked to some of the mahouts who cared for the elephants, and I felt they treated them like family members, they just said that their livelihood depended on these adorable giants. Good or bad, for sure, the elephant parade created a lasting impression on our minds and hearts. Usually, we see an elephant with a mahout nearby, but this was the first time I saw so many elephants walking closely together without a mahout next to each one.

*Lesson # 1:* **You cannot satisfy everyone around you. If you feel your work is good, continue doing it. Do not try to please everyone.**

**"If you want to make everyone happy, don´t be a leader, sell ice creams" – Steve Jobs**

We had our breakfast in a small restaurant facing the river. It was a treat to watch the beauty of the Maha Oya River flowing between its shores. However, the river lost its charm with the grand entry of these majestic creatures. The showtime was over, the elephants returned back to their home after an hour of playtime in the river. We got into our van, were about to leave, we noticed a small souvenir shop, run by the sanctuary, where an array of handcrafted products adorned the shelves, handcrafted greeting cards, papers, boxes, and many other craft items. To our surprise, we learned that they were made from elephant dung. An elephant consumes around 250 kilos of food and excretes about 50 kilos of dung, from which

21

approximately 125 sheets of A4-sized paper were produced. The price was a little on the higher side, but it was worth paying for the noble thought and cause. Like we say that every drop makes an ocean, it was a very small contribution to the fight against global warming, which is a major threat to our planet today.

A piece of advice to fellow travelers and animal lovers, when you venture to new places, whether it be for a pilgrimage or a holiday, make it a point to buy a souvenir. These souvenirs will serve not only as cherished mementos but will also bring back fond memories of your visit when you look at them later. Do not miss the first chance, as there may not be a second.

**Two nights, too many memo(sto)ries** - the real adventure began only then. Though our time at the beaches, hill stations, and the Sigiriya Rock Fortress, believed to be the fort of Ravana, the demon king in the Ramayana, was incredible. It was a scary climb up the rock, I was wonder struck, if it was so scary and risky today, how could have they climbed up and built a fortress, on those days, thousands of years ago. Atop, it was an awe-inspiring view, surrounded by lush green forests. In the distance, I could see a tall white statue of a standing Buddha. There was a Buddha in every corner, much like how one can see a Ganesh on every street in India.

The real adventure began when we visited my childhood friend Vallavan´s home near Sigiriya. Meeting a childhood friend usually involves talking about those wonderful days and playful memories all night long.

However, this visit served two purposes, his house was in a village around the elephant sanctuary, and if you were lucky, you could witness the herds roaming around. It's a different experience altogether to witness wild elephants in their natural habitat.

We started the day with a visit to the nearby elephant sanctuary, it was a thrilling jeep ride through dense forests, finally to an open area around a huge lake. Initially, we saw one or two elephants, but as we neared the lake, we were greeted by the herds grazing in the grasslands. It was a sight to behold. I had never seen elephants in the wild in such numbers in all size from calf to the aged ones. They seemed least bothered by the tourists, they were engrossed in their routine, whether the visitor was a Prime Minister, President or a normal man, they were least concerned who it was, it was the same treatment to all.

> *Lesson # 2:* **Ensure to carry out your tasks with devotion, without being distracted by external circumstances or the people around you.**

> *Lesson # 3:* **Just like the elephants treat the king and soldier with same importance, in your business, make every customer feel important, not only meet their expectations but also exceed them, creating a positive experience that will lead to long-term success.**

## The Wait.

We reached home in the evening. The magic peaked when the sky was painted with dark shades; our discussion slowly turned to the dark-shaded giants. Sitting on the terrace under the portico, my friend mentioned that if we were lucky, we could see elephants roaming around the area. As the village grew darker and people retreated into their houses, we waited for the elephants to emerge. We kept our eyes and ears open, on high alert, waiting for the herds. I remember chasing the Northern lights from Norway to Finland, but this was "waiting for the dark giants" in the nights of Sri Lanka.

My friend, an animal lover like myself, was a living library of knowledge about the animal kingdom. I asked countless questions about the adorable giants, eager to hear it all straight from the horse's mouth. I ended up carrying a treasure trove of stories back from Sri Lanka, which I will share with you on this journey.

The night was pleasant, with gentle winds creating a soft symphony as the branches and leaves brushed against each other, it was sound of music to the ears. I wondered how we would spot these Mr. Blacks on a no moon day. I asked my friend, "When the herd emerges, can you really recognize if it's the same or a different herd, since they all look like the men in black".

This led to a delightful talk about our fascination with color.

**"You are unique"** my friend began. His words were like hitting the nail on the head, creating a wave of thoughts in my mind, like the ripple effect of throwing a stone in a serene lake. He explained that African elephants are heavier and taller than Asian elephants. The most peculiar difference is their ears: African elephants have large ears

24

resembling the shape of the African continent, while Asian elephants have smaller ears with the shape of the Indian subcontinent.

Nature tailors the characteristics of creatures to suit their geographical and climatic contexts. African elephants boast larger ears, crucial for cooling in the continent's hot climate, whereas Asian elephants, in milder temperatures, have smaller ears. Nature knows where different animals live best. Penguins do well in the Arctic, polar bears in the snowy areas, and other bears prefer places that are not too hot or too cold.

Every creature's features serve a purpose, reflecting its lifestyle. It's human constructs like racism, superiority complexes, and societal divides that breed distinctions. Embrace your natural self, as there's a purpose behind every feature, including ear size and skin color for the elephants, dictated by birthplace.

> *"God has designed a unique costume for you,*
> *do not alter it with a local tailor" – BE*

**The craze for color** - The market for fairness creams is substantial in some countries. Before these products could be marketed, initial campaigns aimed to instill the idea that white is pure and black is not. Once this message was implanted in people's minds, the demand for fairness creams grew. Why not embrace the color that God has given to each of us? Animals do not seek to change their colors; only humans do.

*My friend strongly believed in self-love.*

*"Every creation of God is beautiful, you are one of them, believe in it, just fall in love with yourself and everything else will fall in place." – BE*

I asked, "how will everything fall into place if you fall in love with yourself?". He said, "this short story will make it clear to you" and continued.

There's a father with a child excelling in studies, aspiring to become a doctor. However, the father isn't financially sound. What would this father do? Put yourself in his shoes and think of this situation. Would you convince your child to do an arts course and do clerical job or would you go all out to fulfill their dream? Every parent, fueled by love, would move mountains to support their child's aspirations, he would become a Superman or a He-Man to make it happen. Similarly, within each of us lies an inner child. Ask yourself: What does this inner child desire? Dream big, and the father within you will work to fulfill the dreams of the child within you.

Start dreaming today. Set goals with timelines, and the father within you will begin working towards achieving the dreams of the child within you. Start falling in love with yourself from this very moment. Write your dreams on sticky notes, place them where you can see them daily, read them multiple times a day, and you will see things falling into place automatically. Give it a try, it has no cost. Believe it will happen; belief is key.

The story stirred the child within me; I recalled seeing a frame adorning the wall in his room, hung with colorful sticky notes, each bearing his goals and wishes. I went down to his room, to take another look at it, in fact every wall had a story behind in his house.

**Is believing important?** – We went back to the terrace, and I asked him, "Is belief really that important?". Since he´s always been a natural storyteller since childhood, he said, "Let me tell you another story that will make it clearer" and began the next tale.

There was a guy who was having health issues, consulted a Doctor, the Doctor understood that it was due to obesity, said that the God in the temple on top of the mountain near the village is very powerful, that praying to him, the wishes come true, advised him to go to the temple on top of the mountain every day in the morning and pray for good health. After 3 Months, the guy returned with a smile in his face, he looked trim and much better now. He said that the God is very powerful as the Doctor said, he had gone every day without fail and the magic happened, thanked the Doctor with a small gift.

It was the daily walk that had actually did the magic, the temple on top of the mountain was an inspiration, it is the belief that is important. Even when you go to a temple, for a wish to happen, you keep all the faith on the idol that He will grant your wish. It is faith that moves mountains, so you need to believe and have faith in what you do. It is the mind that finally decides whether you want to make things work for you or not. So, first is belief, rest will fall in place automatically. So, go ahead and fall in love with yourself and the magic will happen.

Write your wish in a colorful sticky note, put a date against it, look at it daily, if it does not happen on that date, do not worry, there may be a delay, never a denial. The 12th principle of Buddha is the Law of significance and inspiration, be it big or small, every contribution you make influences the Universe, your positive actions will bring more positivity around you. The cosmic energy around you will bring in the right resources that you will need to make it happen.

So, in conclusion, be proud of who you are. Embrace your color and appearance, as they are features endowed upon you. Just like the shape and size of an elephant's ears vary in different geographical locations, elephants in Africa do not seek to alter the size of their ears, recognizing that their features are determined by God and nature, suited to their environment. Remember, you are a unique creation of God, and there are no design faults in His creation.

Embrace your uniqueness and celebrate the diversity of nature.

You may feel that people born with disabilities are also creations of God, suggesting the existence of "manufacturing defects". Many examples exist of disabled individuals who have excelled, are excelling, and will continue to excel in the future. For instance, consider a man who, after losing a hand in an accident, initially felt despondent but later shined as a champion in White Tiger Kung Fu, a martial art that emphasizes fighting with one hand. Thus, identifying your strengths within your limitations is key to success. It may require some extra time for self-reflection.

Arnold Schwarzenegger faced initial rejection in Hollywood due to his clipped language, large body size, and a name that was not easily pronounceable. Every aspect seemed like a drawback, yet he identified his strengths. Later, these very characteristics became his assets for success. He refused to change his name, pronunciation, or body size. Instead, he perfectly embodied the character required for the movie "Conan the Barbarian" in every aspect, and his journey began.

Elephants are cute in black, though we say that Lord Indira (a Hindu God) has white elephants, think it over on what color will elephants look better, it would probably be the color that they are in now. Stop the craze for color, every color is good, of course white is pure, but black is beautiful.

*Lesson # 4:* **Decorate your room walls with colorful stick notes, detailing your wishes, it will be a daily fuel to your mind to reach your destination, some day. Remember, there may be a delay, never a denial.**

Upon my return to India, this became my Day 1 task, to prepare a frame of stick notes and it's the first thing that I see daily in the morning as soon as I wake up.

## The Tea lesson.

While we were engrossed in conversation, we heard footsteps, it was his dad bringing us tea. Unsure if my question might be inappropriate, but as his childhood friend, I asked why his dad

was serving tea, noting that I typically saw mothers in that role. As we sipped the perfectly brewed aromatic Sri Lankan tea grown locally, my friend explained that in his household, domestic responsibilities are shared without regard to gender norms. Each family member contributes based on capability and availability. Often, his grandfather takes on the cooking, even though his grandmother is present; he believes she has worked hard enough for the family and deserves rest.

***Lesson # 5:* It was a Tea lesson for me, "father has a retirement age, not the mother".**

Elephants are governed by a matriarchal society, similar to many other animal species like the bonobos, whales, ants and bees. Wherever these majestic animals roam, forests thrive, shaped by their movements. Protection of their species remains a primary objective, a trait shared across many species, including humans. Duty allocation within elephant herds is a fascinating display of hierarchical organization: the eldest female leads, and the herd follows her directives unquestioningly, from navigation and predator avoidance to conflict resolution. During rest periods, the herd sleeps together, with a rotating "guard of honor" to alert others of potential dangers. The female leader fosters harmony within the herd, in the face of danger, the eldest elephant, driven by instinctual sacrifice, may willingly offer its life to protect the rest of the herd, exemplifying the innate altruism of these remarkable giants.

*"A leader is best when people barely know he exists, when his work is done, his aim fulfilled, they will say: we did it ourselves."*

***Lao Tzu***

*Lesson #6:* **Elephants epitomize the essence of leadership described in this quote. They quietly carry out their responsibilities, passing down wisdom and guidance to the herd without seeking recognition. Leaders, like the eldest female elephant, to ensure the continuity and well-being of their team, imparting invaluable knowledge gained through experience. True leadership lies in creating opportunities for others, fostering respect, and deserving trust. As you progress in your career, remember to transition from being an individual contributor to a leader, embracing the responsibilities and decisions that come with it.**

*Lesson # 7:* **Be a team player - team building is key to corporate success. In today's world, teamwork is crucial for any organization. Whether in business or sports, victory depends on collaboration. While individual efforts matter, collective unity is essential. Elephants illustrate this well: they stay in herds for survival, predators avoid united herds, showing the strength of togetherness. Similarly, in the corporate world, solidarity and mutual support are vital for success.**

**If an elephant can, can´t we?**

## The gardeners of the forest

As an animal lover who often watches animal-related videos, I believed that elephants were destructive, they break trees, consume a portion of it and leave the rest and they also destroy the grass lands with tons of kilos roaming on it daily. However, my friend changed my perspective, calling them gardeners rather than destroyers. I was wondering how could that be.

Yes, elephants are not just gardeners, but they are guardians of the forest, shaping and nurturing these vital ecosystems. Their actions indirectly benefit forests, essential for the welfare of animals and humans too. Breaking trees provides food and shelter for smaller creatures, and their dung acts as fertilizer, fostering new tree growth. Elephants are true ecosystem engineers, selflessly supporting forest health and wildlife. Their contribution is selfless and effortless, like unpaid gardeners tending to the forest's well-being.

*Lesson # 8:* **Being ethical – every act of the elephant including its poop, is for the betterment of the forest, though it may look like they are destroying greenery, they are being ethical in their actions.**

**I've had the privilege of working with esteemed corporates like the Murugappa and TVS Group of companies early in my career. What struck me most was the emphasis placed on ethics within these organizations. Whether it was internal interactions or external engagements, ethical conduct was paramount. Another concept that left a lasting impression on me was being "easy to do business with." It highlighted the importance of fostering positive and seamless interactions.**

As the Tamil adage says, an elephant is worth a thousand gold coins, whether alive or dead. Just as the elephant benefits its fellow creatures in the forest, strive to be of value to all beings on Earth. Even after you're gone, your teachings can live on.

*Lesson # 9:* **In your workplace, be so valuable that you cannot be ousted from the team, like an elephant is a key role player in the maintenance of the forests, by their actions, lot of other animals around are benefitted, be it finding a water source inside ground, expansion of forest, fertilizing with the dung and many more.**

**Effectively, for a forest to stay a forest, we need these gentle giants. Be a good team player, remember that the team is dependent on your success, and you are dependent on your team's success. Together, you win. In today's scenario, especially in IT profession, people have a fear that they may be laid off, remember that if you are a value to your project, you cannot be laid off easily.**

**Family values.**

Elephants imparts profound lessons for family life, showing extraordinary care for their offspring. It's widely known that encountering an elephant with its calf can be risky, the protective instinct of the elderly elephant towards its young is unmatched. They spare no effort in safeguarding their calves and will fiercely defend them against any perceived threat, leveraging their immense strength if needed.

In human families, amidst rising divorce rates, it's time to remind the duty of parents to nurture and protect their children. I recall a movie dialogue, which says that while husband and wife can divorce, but not a father and mother. If elephants, with their innate understanding of family bonds, prioritize the safety of their calves, shouldn't we humans?

If an elephant can, can't we?

## GNH Vs. GDP.

In Bhutan, I have heard that GNH (Gross National Happiness) is used as an alternative indicator to GDP (Gross Domestic Product) for measuring progress and development. Whether GNH or GDP is considered, the contribution of these gentle giants to both is significant. Tourism industry thrives in many countries based on animals, including Africa and many Asian countries.

Observing animals in their natural habitat is an unforgettable experience that stays with you for a lifetime. There's a world of difference between seeing them in a zoo versus seeing them in wilderness. Elephants, especially, draw countless tourists to destinations like Sri Lanka,

Thailand, Kenya, and India. But watching these majestic creatures in the wilderness is truly awe-inspiring.

Just as tons of weight attract tons of tourists in Africa and Sri Lanka, it's the kilos that draw visitors to Philip Island in Australia, home to the world's largest Little Penguin colony.

Tourists flock to witness the penguin parade. At dusk, the penguins emerged from the sea to return to their burrows. They venture out again at dawn the next day. It was a chill evening, we patiently waited in the gallery, eager for the animal kingdom's VIPs to make their grand entrance. Finally, after nearly an hour, a procession of 20 to 50 penguins swept ashore at a time in batches and they paraded from the shore to their burrows. Whether the elephant parade or the penguin parade, both were mesmerizing sights etched in memory forever.

Wildlife tourism is a booming industry, benefiting sectors like airlines, hotels, and transportation. Africa's diverse wildlife, from elephants to zebras, attracts visitors, especially during events like the wild beast migration in Kenya's Masai Mara and Tanzania's Serengeti.

National Park. Whale and dolphin watching are also popular activities in places like Canada, Iceland, and Australia, offering breathtaking encounters with these marine giants.

India's national parks, such as Gir Forest in Gujarat and Mudhumalai Tiger Reserve in Tamil Nadu, provide opportunities to observe elephants, lions, and tigers in their natural habitats. Spotting these wild animals depends on luck and timing, but persistence pays off for passionate animal lovers.

Apart from their ecological roles, these animals create millions of jobs worldwide. Stay tuned to discover fascinating facts about their economic contributions. It's astonishing to see the financial impact these creatures have on the global economy.

*Lesson # 10*    **Be a guardian angel, like how they contribute selflessly to the growth of the nation, though their primary contribution is to the fellow** beings in the forests. Extend kindness through a warm smile, friendly greeting, or helping hand.

Small gestures have a big impact. At home, in the neighborhood, or at work, strive to spread happiness. Life is precious; choose joy over anger or discontent. Let's make it joyful for ourselves and those around us.

### Truth is stranger than fiction.

My friend took me through a series of serious ups and downs about elephants, from their impact on tourism and GDP to some comical aspects. There are many truths or facts about elephants that seemed stranger than fiction when I heard them. Poachers are typically interested in what's at the front of an elephant: the tusks. But surprisingly, there are also people interested in what's at the back of an elephant. My friend asked if I was confused, and my answer was an obvious yes, he continued.

### Are you a beer lover?

You might have tasted beer made out of fruits, vegetables, nuts, and flowers, but would you prefer to taste beer made out of poop? I can understand the expression on your face, none would. But that wasn't the case; beer manufactured from elephant poop was sold out immediately as soon as it was released.

One of the comments of a beer lover after tasting this beer: *"After downing the last drop, slowly rising from my throat and mouth was that afterglow. The combination of bitter and sweet stayed fresh and lingered in my head. It was a familiar aroma that accompanied me through the entire beer".*

Yes, this happened in Japan. A Japanese brewery by the name of Sankt Gallen manufactured a beer with elephant dung called 'un kono kuru,' which is made using coffee beans that have passed through an elephant. 'Un kono kuru' is a pun on the Japanese word for crap ('unko').

The name has two meanings phonetically: 'Yeah, This Is Black' or 'Shit Black.'

These coffee beans were picked out of elephant excrement, Un, Kono Kuro uses coffee beans taken from heaping piles of crap produced by the gentle giants of Thailand's Golden Triangle Elephant Foundation. Sold for about 10,000 yen (US$104) per 35 grams as Black Ivory, the beans are fed to the elephants, pass through their entire digestive system, and are shat out undigested and served to your doorstep.

This product was a one-time sale; it did not hit the shelves in the market due to the cost involved. It was expensive to feed and maintain the elephants. It's an expensive process as 33 kg of beans in the mouth yields about 1 kg out the other end.

**Are you a coffee lover?**

Not only for beer lovers, but there is also coffee as well made out of elephant poop, called the black ivory coffee, exclusively produced by Thai elephants, coffee cherries are mixed and fed to the elephants and the bean from the poop are harvested to produce a different taste.

Food products, not just from elephants' poop are expensive and tasty, there are others too, let us look at some.

**Kopi luwak coffee - also called civet coffee in the West.**

Do you know that 'kopi luwak coffee' is one of the best coffees in the world? One cup of kopi luwak coffee costs around $35 to $80. Read on to know why it is so expensive and why it tastes so great. It's a kind of drink made from coffee beans that are excreted whole by an animal called a civet cat, even though civet cats do not belong to the cat family. These animals are very choosy about the type of coffee cherries they consume.

Native farmers grow the coffee plants. Ripe coffee cherries from the plants are fed to the civet cats. Within 24 to 36 hours, the gastric juices from the civet's digestive system change the taste and chemical composition of the coffee beans. After the digestion process, the civet will excrete partially digested coffee beans. The coffee beans are then handpicked from the excrement and processed, this includes washing, drying, and roasting. The kopi luwak beans are packaged and sold.

In simpler words, it's cat poop coffee.

**Bat Coffee**

In the quaint lands of Costa Rica, amidst the rustling palms and whispering winds, there exists a brew unlike any other, made from poop of bat, though called so, they are not from their poop, but they are the cherries that are nibbled by the bats. It's a brew steeped in mystery and charm, whispered about in hushed tones among those who seek the rare and exotic.

## Coffee from bird's poop

In the sun-kissed lands of Brazil, where coffee plantations stretch as far as the eye can see, there exists a brew of unparalleled allure, the Jacu bird coffee. These winged wonders, with their discerning taste, gracefully partake of the ripest coffee cherries. Rather than shooing them away, the planters gather the seeds from their droppings, cherishing the unique blend of nutty and honeyed flavors it imparts. It's a tradition steeped in harmony with nature, yielding a brew cherished by connoisseurs far and wide.

## Monkey coffee

Again, not from the poop, but from the seeds tenderly savored by the Rhesus monkeys of Taiwan and India, are harvested. The coffee made from these seeds, infused with the monkeys' saliva, boasts a distinct taste profile loved by many. These monkeys choose the seeds themselves, unlike the civet cats, which are forcefully fed.

## Poop Paper

We had already seen the handicrafts made from elephant dung at the Pinnawala Elephant Sanctuary. I salute the person who planted the seeds for this noble idea. Just as the Nobel Prize recognizes achievements in science and peace, these small but impactful inventions also deserve recognition, is my humble opinion.

## Can one person kill 40,000 elephants?

It was almost eleven in the night, with every mention of a product made from poop, though it elicited laughter, my eyes remained vigilant for the herds to emerge from the forests, and my ears were keen for the sound of their trumpets. We took a walk around the terrace to look in all directions, when my friend asked, "Can one person kill 40,000 elephants?" I was stunned. "What? Are you kidding? How could that be true?" It sounded improbable, even in the context of ancient battles where elephants were used, but the idea of one person killing 40,000 elephants was still very strange.

It is disheartening to hear this statement itself, isn't it? Yes, one man killed 40,000 elephants. His name is Allan Savory, an Ecologist in Africa.

In the 1950s, Savory helped create large national parks in Africa. But as people left this land to make way for animal reserves, Savory and his team noticed the land deteriorating and quickly turning into desert. After careful analysis, they determined that the problem was an over-abundance of elephants. And so, in a politically heated move, they shot 40,000 elephants in order to save the grasslands. Even with all these elephants killed, the grassland deterioration only got worse.

I recall vividly the day I was on my bike in a highway when, unexpectedly, a puppy darted into my path, resulting in me injuring the pup, with too many stray dogs in a country like India, such encounters are regrettably unavoidable at times. This distressing event happened some

25 years ago, continues to haunt my memory still at times with feelings of sadness and guilt. So, you can imagine the state of this individual, it was not merely one or two, but a staggering forty thousand elephants that met their untimely demise as a result of ignorance and neglect. In a powerful moment in the talk, Savory expresses his dismay. "That was the saddest and greatest blunder of my life, I will carry that to my grave" he said.

*"யான் செய்த தவறு செய்யாமல்*
*இருக்கட்டும் இவ்வையகம்"*

***"May those who follow not tread the same paths of error I once did." – BE.***

## Elephant friendly honey

In the wilds of Africa, there's a struggle between people and elephants. The elephant numbers have dropped a lot, but humans keep increasing. Both need the same things: space and food.

It is said that the elephant's population has become one third over a period of time and human population has quadrupled over the same period of time. Elephants often wander into villages and farms looking for food, causing conflicts. To keep them out, people put up electric fences. Sometimes, these fences harm both elephants and humans. But elephants are clever, they find ways to crawl under the fences. So, while some folks try to harm elephants out of ignorance, others work hard to protect them.

41

After careful observation, it became evident that elephants held a deep fear of bees. They avoided any tree with a beehive, refraining from disturbing it for food, a behavior typically seen as they journeyed through the forest. Remarkably, this wisdom was passed down through generations, with matriarchs teaching younger elephants to steer clear of bee-infested trees.

Curious researchers tested this phenomenon by playing recorded bee sounds near resting elephant herds. The elders, recognizing the danger, swiftly alerted the others, prompting a rapid retreat. In their haste, the elephants even threw sand to ward off potential bee attacks. Repeat experiments with different herds yielded consistent results, inspiring a novel solution.

Watch the video to see the reaction of the elephants to the sound of bees, and you cannot stop laughing seeing it, it is so cute on the way they recognize the sound and react to it.

Artificial beehives, alternating between real and dummy ones, were strategically placed using ordinary ropes, not electrified fences, to deter elephants from crop areas and villages. This ingenious method proved highly effective, safeguarding both elephants and crops at minimal cost and without harm.

The honey harvested from these hives, branded as "Elephant Friendly Honey" became a valuable commodity, providing additional income for locals. Beeswax from the hives was also utilized to craft candles, creating a new source of revenue and further promoting harmony between humans and elephants. Additionally, the bees aided crop pollination, offering yet another benefit to the community.

## Tusk less elephants.

In the vast plains of Africa, both male and female elephants proudly bear their tusks, though males boast larger and longer tusks. These ivory treasures serve as indispensable tools for elephants, similar to hands for humans, aiding them in breaking branches to access water and minerals beneath the earth's surface. This resourcefulness not only sustains the elephants but also nurtures the ecosystem, providing water and nourishment for other creatures in the forest.

Tragically, the allure of ivory has driven these majestic creatures to the brink of extinction. Despite valiant efforts by animal protection groups, illegal ivory trade persists. Initially, poachers targeted male elephants for their imposing tusks, but as populations dwindled, females with smaller tusks fell victim to the same fate. In recent years, a startling trend emerged, elephants are born without tusks. Reports from Addo Elephant National Park in the early 2000s revealed that a staggering 98 percent of female elephants were tuskless. This remarkable adaptation suggests a profound shift in elephant behavior, a collective response to the relentless threat of poaching. Studies now scrutinize the behavior of tusked and tuskless elephants, pondering whether their movements differ.

According to the Buddha's law of karma, it is believed that through sustained focus, individuals can manifest certain outcomes in their lives, but it is astonishing that these creatures can alter their physical structure with their strong thought process, to protect their future generations from falling prey to poaching.

Studies say that the structure of elephants has evolved over a period of time. Millions of years ago, it is believed that they had tusks but no trunks. So, with today's scenario, we may see the elephants evolving further with trunks and no tusks.

My friend added that there is some good created by nature to the elephants of Sri Lanka, they do not have much tusks, due to which, poaching does not happen much.

**Lesson # *11:* The make it happen attitude – It's the responsibility of the leader to ensure success for both the organization and its followers at any cost. Consider the remarkable adaptation of the tuskless elephants, evolving in response to the threats from poaching, in being able to shape their very physiology. Similarly, a leader must possess the make it happen attitude to steer the organization to success.**

**If an elephant can, can´t we?**

### Humans were once cannibals; can they still be?

My friend asked me a strange question if I would ever turn to be a cannibal, to which my answer was a definite no and he took me through another story of cannibalism, every story he narrated, took me to the verge of curiosity.

Elephants and many monkeys are herbivores, living solely on plants, vegetables, and fruits. My mother used to advocate vegetarianism, emphasizing the value of not harming other beings for personal satisfaction. She pointed out that elephants, incredibly strong animals, are strict vegetarians, as are other formidable creatures like the monkeys. Even in times of drought when food is scarce, herbivores like elephants stick to their plant-based diet, refusing to resort to hunting other animals. On the other hand, carnivores like lions and tigers exclusively consume meat. Animals adhere to their natural instincts and do not deviate from their dietary habits.

Humans, however, possess the ability to adapt drastically to survive. An example of extreme adaptation occurred in 1972 when a rugby team's plane crashed in the Andes mountains, killing 29 and 16 survived. Stranded survivors resorted to cannibalism; they ate the flesh of the dead in order to survive for nearly 72 days. While cannibalism dates back thousands of years, it serves as a reminder of humanity's potential to revert to primal instincts in dire circumstances.

## The wandering elephants of China.

Elephants, like many animals, stick to familiar paths passed down through generations. These routes, ingrained in their instincts, ensure they navigate safely through their environment. Such behavior is not unique to elephants; migrating birds, for instance, follow regular routes over vast distances.

*Lesson # 12:* **Standard Operating Procedures or SOP's. We've all heard it countless times, especially in the IT industry but applicable to all sectors, the importance of documenting and adhering to SOPs. Yet, even after hearing it repeatedly, we often**

**discover errors, prompting us to refine our processes further.**

**Elephants, across millions of years, have passed down their SOPs through generations, from their established paths to foraging techniques without the aid of pen, paper, technology or language. If elephants can do it without a document, can´t we humans do it with a document?**

However, in a rare occurrence, a herd of 15 elephants embarked on an unprecedented journey from Xishuangbanna National Nature Reserve in southern China. Over 17 months, they traveled 500 kilometers, giving birth to two calves along the way and they were back on their journey in just 2 days, taking a short break.

*Lesson # 13:* **Be a quick learner - Elephants are smart & quick learners. A baby elephant can stand in just 20 minutes and walk in 2 hours. Within 2 days, they join their herd, always on the move together. Humans take much longer to stand or walk, but the lesson is clear: be quick to learn and keep moving forward.**

*Lesson # 14:* **An idle mind is a devil´s workshop - Elephants never sit still, they're always on the move, even when stationed in one place. It's a reminder that our bodies are meant to move, not to remain stagnant. In today's world, many of us lead sedentary lifestyles, especially IT professionals, which leads to health issues.**

**But observing elephants, we see creatures of immense size constantly on the move, if an animal**

**weighing tons can be active, can´t we? Keep your mind and body on the move always, never idle.**

Despite efforts to redirect them, one male elephant was captured, while the rest returned to their original habitat by September 2021. Their journey captivated social media, with many marveling at the "cute" explorers. Yet, behind the fascination lay a complex situation feel some researchers. The elephants inadvertently caused damage to crops along their route, prompting government initiatives to protect both the herd and affected communities. Special teams with drones monitored their movements around the clock.

During their journey, remarkable displays of intelligence were witnessed. One elephant operated a tap to access water, showcasing a level of problem-solving ability. An elderly member of the herd intervened to resolve a conflict between two others, demonstrating social awareness and leadership. Meanwhile, another elephant stood guard while the rest slept, exemplifying a sense of communal protection.

Additionally, villagers exhibited compassion by prioritizing the safety of the elephants over potential crop damage. This collective effort underscored the harmonious relationship between humans and wildlife in the face of unexpected challenges. While the elephants´ adventure may have been a one-time event, it left a lasting impression on those who witnessed it. The herd´s return to their habitat marked the end of an extraordinary journey, reminding us of the intelligence and adaptability of these magnificent creatures.

*Lesson # 15:* **Embrace change – Embrace risk. They normally follow their herd path, yet elephants possess a remarkable openness to change. The leader in the wandering herds of China demonstrated its readiness to venture into new territories, to try something new. Similarly, a leader must embody this spirit of exploration, constantly seeking uncharted paths and new horizons. When a novel idea strikes, seize the moment and take action without delay, for time waits for none. Trust your instincts, for they often lead you correctly. Embrace risk, success puts you a step ahead and failure teaches you a valuable lesson.**

*Lesson # 16:* **Communication is key to success, elephants are great communicators, even over long distances. Experiments with wandering elephants in China revealed the herd's ability to communicate though they were miles away from the isolated male elephant, indicating a sophisticated means of communication.**

**Additionally, they utilize seismic signals, detecting vibrations through the ground, to communicate with each other.**

**Effective communication is not just essential in corporate houses; it's vital in every aspect of life, from family relationships to educational environments. Remember that communication is essential to even a beggar, unless he is able to**

**effectively communicate his need, he will not get his meal for the day.**

## The return to the forests

"Return to the forest", is a Royal initiative of Her Majesty Queen Sirikit of Thailand, it's mission is to reintroduce captive elephants back to the wild in three vast protected forest habitats within Thailand where there is no tourism. The queen was an animal lover, especially elephants and hence this initiative, it is the giant love of the queen towards the gentle giants.

## Logical thinking of elephants.

Research conducted on elephants in Thailand by Dr. Josh Plotnik sheds light on how animals cooperate for mutual benefit. Similar findings have been observed in studies on primates.

These animals demonstrate remarkable cooperation, employing logical and mathematical thinking to act in unison for mutual gain.

In one experiment, a rope was attached to a box of fruit, with two chimpanzees holding the ends. They synchronized their efforts to pull the rope, bringing the box closer to enjoy the fruits together. They even demonstrated an understanding that pulling alone would result in the rope slipping off the box, showing logical problem-solving skills. Another test involved one chimp being already fed, while the other was not. Despite this, the unfed chimp managed to convince its companion to pull the rope, displaying their ability to value relationships and cooperate for shared benefit.

Observing these behaviors in both videos highlights the impressive teamwork of chimps and elephants. However, in the final elephant test, one clever elephant opted to stay idle while its companion worked, reaping the benefits alone – a behavior not uncommon in office environments, where some may slack off while others shoulder the workload.

**Stories from Africa.**

Africa is steeped in tales of elephants, passed down through generations via oral tradition, the practice of honoring the deceased is not unique to humans; animals, too, demonstrate rituals of respect. When a member of an elephant herd passes away, the remaining elephants engage in a solemn ritual to honor the departed. They pause in their journey to pay their respects, standing in reverent silence at the site of the loss. This poignant display likely serves as a moment of homage, allowing them to reflect on their fallen comrade before carrying on with their journey.

Stories abound of elephants retrieving the bones of their fallen kin, presumably killed by humans, and solemnly returning them to the site of death for burial. Additionally, there are accounts of elephants venturing into villages, targeting only the individual responsible for the harm caused to their herd mate, displaying a remarkable sense of justice and vengeance.

**The wait was over, did we see the elephants?**

The time was almost 2:00 in the morning, we rose from our sitting posture for one last time, to see if we could see the dark giants in the darkest of night, but to our vain, the herd never emerged from the forest that night. Being an animal lover who has patiently waited to spot wildlife in various places, I know that sighting an animal is often a matter of luck. It's like playing in a casino, it only clicks if luck is on your side. That was not my day, this is something very common that happens to animal lovers, but we never stop, there is always a next time.

The wait was over, and we decided to go to sleep since we had to get to the sanctuary the next morning. Early mornings are usually the best time to sight animals. Though I've shared some of the stories my friend from Sri Lanka narrated, there were countless lessons from these gentle giants that weigh in tons. Upon my return, I compiled these learnings and now share them with you with the phrase, "If an elephant can, can't we?".

**My personal experience with this adorable giant.**

Can you get near to a well grown elephant and play with it like you would with your pet dog? It sounds scary, doesn't it? Let me share my personal experience with an elephant.

It is a common sight to see folks keeping dogs or cats as pets. However, the notion of having an elephant as a household companion was an entirely different matter altogether. Such a venture carried a weighty burden, both in terms of literal weight and financial expense. Feeding an elephant required a staggering amount of sustenance, with the majestic creature consuming around 250 kilos of food each day, alongside copious amounts of water for both consumption and bathing rituals.

One of my friends, Madhan, hailing from the ancient city of Madurai in Tamil Nadu, descends from a lineage of mahouts for many generations. They have an elephant named Sumathi in their house, and our visits to Madhan's house were to spend time with Sumathi rather than Madhan.

Normally, you can only observe an elephant from a distance in a temple or zoo. The mahouts, due to the size and strength of this adorable giant, maintain a cautious distance between the animal and us. But it was different with Sumathi; with Madhan around, we could play with her like any other pet you may have at home. On a Friday, we used to take a bus or train from Chennai to Madurai, arriving at his home in the morning around 6:00, to spend the whole weekend with Sumathi.

The morning began with a leisurely stroll to a nearby tea shop, where we enjoyed tea, with Sumathi also joining us. I still remember how Madhan parked her like a vehicle among other vehicles, giving instructions to move forward, left, reverse, and voila, she was parked. It was like a parallel parking experience. Later, we would go around in a tricycle, fetching greenery for her morning breakfast. The highlight of the day was bathing time with splashes and laughter, some of us brushing her trunks, some attending to her legs, and some atop her, scrubbing her back. Then we would prepare lunch and feed her, and we would have lunch as well, sitting beside her. Later in the evening, we would decorate her like a bride and take her for an evening walk, allowing her to graze in the grasslands nearby. We would play with her for some time, carrying tea and snacks, with her getting her share too. Then, again, we would feed her some fruits at night, and at times, we would sleep next to her in a rope cot. I have sat watching Sumathi sleep. She would be the first one to wake us up in the morning, putting her trunk on our head and face.

*Lesson # 17:* **Sleep peacefully, however your day was, good or bad, to sleep peacefully is important.**

The times spent with Sumathi were one of the best in my life, I would carry this experience until my grave. Thanks to Madhan, if not for him, I would have never known the love of this gentle giant and thanks a ton to the 4 ton Sumathi. We love you Sumathi.

*Lesson # 18:* **Right today, right now – take a pen & paper (later transfer it to stick notes), write what you will do differently this year and next year – apart from your regular routine. It may be to spend time with an animal, go on a solo road trip, do mountaineering, go for a mountain trek – something different. Do certain things while you have the age and energy.**

**Goodbye Sri Lanka.**

My walk along the elephant path, alongside the gentle giant, with every step, led me to a world of lessons. It was not just a herd path but a path to enlightenment, advancing both professionally and personally. With this, let's embark on a journey of discovery, exploring the invaluable lessons they offer, from the perspective of companies striving for success to the individual seeking personal growth. All good and bad things have to come to an end, and my trip to Sri Lanka, a good thing of course, was no exception. I left with loads of stories and memories. A big thank you to my childhood friend Vallavan.

The strong lesson that went into my mind was – if an elephant can, can´t we?

*"இருந்தாலும் ஆயிரம் பொன்னே,*
*இறந்தாலும் நீ ஆயிரம் பொன்னே*
*கயமுனியே"*

*"You are worth a thousand gold coins, alive or dead, my dear elephant"*

*- Be Happy Always –*

❧

# The V (We) Secret of Birds

*"You cannot perform without the team and the team cannot perform without you"*

Y ou cannot learn the secret of the word "WE (V)" from anyone else better than the birds.

It was an early Saturday morning; the alarm rang at 6:00am. I pressed the snooze button and went back to sleep. In five minutes, the alarm rang again, and I hit snooze one more time.

There's something incredibly satisfying about those extra five minutes of sleep, it feels like diving into deep sleep within seconds, bringing immense pleasure.

I was at the house of my school friend Manimaran's, in Kodaikanal (a beautiful hill station in south of India) on that day. My friend was born and brought up in the hills, he had been calling me for quite long and the day had arrived to visit him. We both had similar interests, he was another animal lover like me, but he was a little more or different than me in some or rather many ways, he was another library of knowledge about the animal kingdom. I can spend whole day and night, watching an elephant, a cow or any animal for that matter, but with a bird was something strange to me. One of Manimaran's hobby was bird watching, he has travelled across various remote areas for bird watching. It sounded strange to me to sit beneath a tree for hours together to watch a bird take off from its nest, but he was one of those types. Though I love feeding the crows and pigeons, watching them for hours was something new. He could even tell the species by hearing to the sound of those birds.

Manimaran woke me up saying we have to start early, the plan was a 2 day trek from Kodaikanal to Mannavanur, with a night stay in a self-erected tent at Berijam lake.

Few more of his bird watching friends joined and finally there were 15 of us, we had to carry tents, sleeping bags, stove and food, so everyone had a luggage to carry, some of them had huge binoculars hanging like a garland in their neck. I was thrilled to be part of that team, it was a different experience for me, having born and brought up in a city, this was a new experience closer to nature. we had packed some bread and omelet for breakfast and started off on our journey, objective was to have a trekking experience through the forests and to get to see some native birds.

The trek was an unforgettable experience. My friend's house was atop a hill in the outskirts of Kodai, surrounded by lush green valleys. We began our journey and as we started to walk, watching the breath-taking view of the valleys, slowly we were entering into the forest range, with towering trees above us, though the Sun was making the sky brighter with its rise, the area was becoming darker with the dense trees above us. As we ventured deeper, the sound of civilization faded away slowly, replaced with the sound of birds and the branches of the trees brushing against each other. The air was much more cool and pure, the smell of the damp soil and wet leaves on it, the fragrance of the wild herbs was aromatic. The valley views kept appearing and disappearing, with the sudden flow of mist, not just the valleys, we could hardly see only few meters ahead of us, it gave a feel like we were in Cloud 9.

Manimaran was enthusiastic, sharing stories of his previous birdwatching experiences. His excitement was contagious, making me excited too. I didn't know what to expect, but my inner self felt something interesting was going to happen in the next 2 days to come. Upon arriving at a beautiful viewpoint, it was a cliff, where we could see a huge silent valley in front of our eyes, we stopped for a tea break, which we had brough in flasks. Every sip of the hot tea with a chill breeze hitting your lips at the same time, gave a different taste to the local tea.

We continued our journey, into the dense forest, the sound of birds was intense in the morning as there were too many in the trees above us. I just closed my eyes and I was taken back to the days I used to live in an ashram in my younger days after college, all the streets were surrounded by dense trees, providing home to the birds and shelter to the pedestrians. There was never a need for an alarm then, the melodious chorus of thousands of birds naturally woke us up daily at 4:00 AM. In ashrams, there are no conventional classrooms with textbooks and chalkboards, instead, life's most profound lessons unfold through daily living, and the surroundings are such that you learn everything through the lifestyle itself. With nature's alarm clocks echoing through the trees, there was no need for separate alarm clock. It made me wonder in those days how do these birds wake up on time with no alarm clocks ringing near their ears.

I always believed in time machines, like the one in movies like "Back to the Future." You may be surprised and think it's impossible and it´s just imagination. But let me tell you, time machines do exist. The sound of these birds took me back to my younger days. A close of my eyes, and I felt I was in my old house, standing on the balcony, hearing the same sounds.

Sometimes, during a travel or in a tea shop, you might hear a song on the radio that reminds you of your childhood days, a relationship or a crush that you might have had in your school. A close of your eyes, and it's like re-living those days. Yes, in my view, time machines exist.

You may not physically travel, but virtually – it's a definite yes, today was one such day for me. Suddenly, my friend held my hand and the time machine brought me back to the hills.

## A true world wonder.

As we walked, Manimaran suddenly held my hand and pointed to a treetop where a small bird was gathering sticks to build its home. He offered his binoculars and suggested we sit quietly

to observe. The bird laid the sticks, flew away, and returned with another piece, in the midst of collecting materials. He asked if I had ever tried building a nest. My answer was an obvious "no", why would I? That's for birds. But he insisted I try to build one sometime, to understand the intricacies.

Can you imagine a single individual embodying the roles of builder, supplier, engineer, architect, technician, quality analyst, worker, and homeowner? Not easily feasible, but these birds seamlessly fulfill all these functions. They go around their surroundings for optimal building materials, grass & sturdy leaves for the nest's base, similarly sized sticks for structure, soft leaves for comfort and flexible strong strings to tie them up.

Ensuring the nest is well- placed among the branches, capable of withstanding wind and rain. Some birds, like the weaver birds (தூக்கணங்குருவி), go further, creating multi-chambered nests with entry protection against predators capturing fireflies to illuminate the nest's inner walls.

Try it sometime, collect these materials, attempt to build a small nest, and place it in a tree. You'll quickly realize the challenge of crafting something sturdy and protective with such simple materials and attempt to tie a knot with just one hand and you will know how difficult a task it is for a bird with just its beaks. Then you'll appreciate the architectural knowledge and capacities of these small birds.

He added that these are true world wonders more than the Taj Mahal and the Eiffel Tower, which I felt like agreeing. My bird watching experience was becoming more and more interesting getting to know about these engineering marvels, putting up a firefly within the inner walls for illuminating the chamber is a super thought. Weaver birds - they are the Edisons of the bird family. Later, upon my return, I did attempt to build a nest and miserably failed, but it was a humbling experience.

*Lesson #1:* **Give it a try, attempt to build a nest with sticks, leaves and features. Try to tie a knot with one hand using all 5 fingers to make the nest stand in a tree and you will know how big the small bird is and how small are you, though big. We can easily ask the question "if such a small bird can, can´t** we?", it's easy to ask this question, but very difficult to answer.

**Marriages are made in heaven.**

It was almost afternoon, and we were in a huge open area with a small lake in the middle. Silence surrounded us, and the only sounds we could hear were the 'creech' of insects and an occasional bird cooing. I was thinking over the path we had treaded, the open stretch leaving the village behind, then into the woods, cliffs, valleys and the mountain ranges, now we were here in the midst of the forest, if I were left here alone for some reason, the return back home would not be possible, because, it looked all the same trees on all sides and there are no sign boards in the forests. Unless you are familiar with the place, you cannot come out of the forests. Similar is what I observed in the deserts in the Middle East, during the desert safari trips, you will have a 4 wheel motor bike to take a short ride, you will be advised not to go too far, because, it will be sand on all sides and with the wind, the tyre marks will be gone as well, and you will be lost in the desert. I felt that these forests were similar, it looks the same on all directions, that you will never be able to find your way back if lost, so holding on to your guide is very important in these adventure trips.

*Lesson # 2:* **Once you take up any task, ensure you only go forward with it. Some people start a business having a backup plan, in case it fails, so that you have something to fall back in case of a failure. When getting into business, you should step into with a firm belief that there is no backup plan,**

61

**there is only one plan, which is to go forward. Even in software upgrade or any major activity in the IT industry, we take a backup before the activity, but when faced with issues, we always try to go with a fix forward, rarely do we revert the old backup. There are many cases where people who have been thrown out of their jobs, started business and succeeded, because they knew that there is no other way, the only way is to succeed in what they have started.**

We had our lunch and continued further, we had to cross shallow waters, and there were hundreds of leaches everywhere and they were sticking on to our foot, they literally suck the blood out of you slowly. So, as soon as we crossed that area we had to take a sharp stick and remove them from our skin. My friend said that its no harm as far as you remove them, he added that they are used for medical purpose to remove blood clot or to remove bad blood. It was initially scary but got used to it.

Walking past the open space, the stretch ahead of us looked steep, it was a zig zag route to the top, with a slight slip will take you right to the bottom. Having taken the step to trek through the forests, there was no giving up possible.

We reached the top and a look at the steep path we had treaded was scary, Manimaran continued, shared another fascinating fact about birds and nests. In today's world, marriage expectations have evolved: gone are those days of boys placing demands. Today, girls demand that the boy has his own house, car, and a hefty bank balance, though an evolving trend in humans, this practice has been followed by birds for ages. Weaver birds, select mates based on nest-building skills. Males construct nests and invite females, the female inspects them for comfort and safety, if satisfied, the craftsmanship is rewarded with partnership. However, if a male fails to impress, it dismantles the nest fully and starts anew, aiming to build a better abode next time and to impress a new partner.

Now that the nest is complete and approved by the female partner, life begins for this new pair of weaver birds. Unlike fairy tales that often conclude with the phrase "and they lived happily ever after", their journey isn't that smooth. They face numerous challenges, battling rain and wind, evading predators, and confronting the greatest threat of all: human hunters. As my friend explained the life of a bird, I felt grateful for what I am.

*Lesson # 3:*

*from the lines of Kannadasan:*
*"உனக்கும் கீழே உள்ளவர் கோடி,*
*நினைத்து பார்த்து நிம்மதி நாடு"*
*"There are so many below you;*
*be grateful for what you have."*

**The first flight**

Manimaran said that he has spent days waiting under trees to witness the first flight of birds, a task that requires a lot of patience and helps to build patience itself. They setup camera atop the tree with a view of the nest and keep observing. He said that the female remains at the nest during pregnancy while the male hunts for food. After the eggs hatch, one parent stays in the nest to protect the young from predators and the other forages for food. The young ones gradually open their eyes to the world, nurtured by their parents until they mature. Rising before dawn becomes a natural habit learned from their parents, eliminating the need for alarm clocks or snooze buttons. Eventually, these tiny creatures take their first flight into the sky, marking a significant milestone in their lives.

The first flight of a bird is a profound moment in its life, giving it a sense of exploration and freedom. With each flutter of their wings, they ascend higher into the sky, experiencing the thrill of flight. It's a transformative moment for the young bird as it realizes its ability to soar high above trees, mountains, and seas, through clouds, and even above rains if they are eagles. Manimaran said it was a fascinating experience, not just for the young bird but also for him, to watch it flutter its wings, descend and ascend in its first flight, the fluttering sound was like music to the ears.

I was reminded of the day I first rode my bicycle, mastering the art of balancing on two wheels. Though a comfortable ride today, the first ride was a thrilling experience, it was a multitasking experience, I could pedal, steer, look ahead, and control my speed all at once. I remembered how I used to fall to the right or left, but this time I didn't fall; instead, I pedaled faster, smoothly riding on a thin layer of rubber connecting me to the ground. For parents as well, it's a sensational moment to watch their children balance a bicycle for the first time, a feel-good moment seeing them become independent. It's a similar moment for a young bird

on its maiden flight and for the bird parent, marking the beginning of a new journey filled with endless possibilities and adventures.

> *Lesson #2:* **What a moment it must have been for your dad or mom, watching you balance the bicycle on your own for the first time. When was the last time you gave them such a feeling, and when will be the next time? Grab a sticky note, right now, jot down how and when you'll make it happen next. Look at it daily and you will see it materializing.**

## The great migrations.

As we were talking, we noticed a V shape high in the sky. It might have been a coincidence, but it led us to another round of exciting information about migration. I vaguely knew that birds fly in this shape to gain energy from each other, but I did not know there was an ocean of secrets behind this V.

The birds that fly in a V shape are mostly migratory birds. The younger ones undergo extensive training with their parents, mastering the art of long-distance flight over thousands

of miles. They learn intricate routes, knowing precisely when to turn left or right, where to rest, and where to find essential resources like food and water. They're taught the destination, the duration of their stay, the return timing, and the exact route back to their starting point without the aid of door numbers, street names, cities, or postal codes.

It's like a yearly tour package or a pilgrimage trip, passed down from generation to generation. Remarkably, these avian travelers navigate without compasses, GPS, or Google Maps, yet they unfailingly arrive at their destination each year, right on schedule. This demonstrates their natural know-how and impressive skills developed over many generations of migration.

Then, my friend asked another strange question, "Can you teach a bird to fly, to migrate?" Once again, the answer was an obvious "No." He continued, "It sounds strange, doesn't it? Yet, it has happened", It was as strange as to say "teaching a fish to swim".

It was a different experience, to adjust the binoculars to view some of the birds very close, it was a like a little wonder, some with very strange colors, not sure which artist has thrown so many colors into this little being. I was inquisitive and asked further about migration.

Manimaran said it is a long story that cannot be cut short and promised to start afresh when we crossed the steep mountain range, as we had to give all our attention only to the path. It was all ups and downs, just like our life, it was difficult climbing up but the down was easy. So is life, building trust is difficult, takes time, but destroying it needs no effort, takes just a minute.

I was eager to hear the story of migrations, feeling rather impatient and worried we might forget and miss out on his personal experiences. Yet, I reminded myself to be patient. He was part of a group of bird lovers who walk into forests with drones to observe nests from an aerial view, waiting below trees for the magical moment to happen. His patience, humility, and politeness were evident. Waiting hours to watch a bird for a few seconds, you inevitably develop lot of patience over time. This bird-watching experience was a lesson in patience, and it was worth the visit. I decided to wait for him to start on his own.

## The aviation experts.

Birds are the real aviation experts, how a bird migrates all the way from Australia to India is a mystery, how do they decide what date to start, how is the communication done to all the birds, what time do they start, which route do they take, where do they rest in between, because it is all vast stretches of open sky and ocean all along, where do they get food and water during this travel, how do they get to know which exit to take to reach India in this long journey. It was making me wonder more and more thinking more about it. Manimaran explained, like how we have sign boards in roads, explaining which route or exit to take to reach our destination, they have their own way of identifying landmarks, birds rely heavily on earth's magnetic forces, as well as the positions of the sun, moon, and stars, for navigation.

They do not depend on human made landmarks, as they may keep changing over time, so they depend on natural landmarks such as mountains and rivers.

Today, with the growth in aviation technology, our pilots can put flights in auto mode, simply overseeing the altitude and speed. Manimaran has flown in small jets with a friend whose hobby is flying jets. He mentioned that at a certain point, both the sky and the sea look the same shade of blue, making it hard to know if you're heading in the right direction. With high- flying jets, technology makes navigation easier. But it's a wonder that birds navigate these challenges effortlessly, avoiding potential mishaps and ensuring successful migrations.

Birds are remarkable flying machines, equipped with approximately 20,000 feathers that serve as their natural propellers for takeoff and landing. Their legs act as built-in landing gears, facilitating smooth landings. Interestingly, the design of airplanes has been inspired by the aerodynamic principles observed in birds.

In a remarkable display of self-care, birds engage in "overhauling" by applying wax from a gland on their rear to their feathers. This process renders their plumage waterproof, flexible, and resistant to parasites. Given the critical importance of proper maintenance for their long migratory flights, birds meticulously attend to their grooming routine to avoid exhaustion.

The mystery lies in how birds acquire such intricate knowledge of self-maintenance and flight mechanics. Additionally, like humans, birds also engage in leisure activities to unwind. At times, they are seen "surfing" through the air, like how a pilot's announces on a flight to "sit back, relax, and enjoy the journey.

**The number game.**

Manimaran said that birding does a lot of good, it allows you to connect with nature more closely, develop patience, make you humbled and asked if I wanted to know about birds and numbers, I thought it was something like numerology, but it was a different number game.

| | |
|---|---|
| **Number 1** | The number of eyes that a ducks keeps it open while sleeping. |
| **Number 2 ¼ inches** | The length of the smallest bird on Earth, called bee hummingbird. |
| **Number 20** | 20% of birds population are long distance migratory birds |
| **Number 43** | The speed of ostrich is 43 miles per hour. |
| **Number 50** | Number of words a parrot can learn. |
| **Number 100** | Number of words an African gray parrot can learn. |
| **Number 10,000** | The estimated number of bird species that exist. |
| **Number 150 million** | The number of years since birds have existed in this planet, since the period of dinosaurs, yes, since the Jurassic period. |

**The cunning crow.**

We've all heard stories about the cleverness of crows, but are they really cunning? The truth is they are actually very intelligent and innocent. I have heard my parents tell me the story of a crow dropping stones into a pot to raise the water level and drink it. I believed it as a child, but later thought it was just a story meant to inspire me to think creatively. Much later, I came to know that these stories aren't just stories but real. In lab experiments, crows have been observed selecting sinking objects to raise water levels in containers. In another test, they used curved sticks to extract food from a tricky container. This proves that crows have complex problem-solving skills.

As we kept walking, we heard a strange sound of a bird. Manimaran silenced us and asked us to listen more carefully. He said it was from a particular species of bird. I was surprised that he could identify the bird by its sound. He said that one would learn over time, especially when with groups of bird watchers. He then shared a scary experience he once had during a bird- watching trip in Sri Lanka. He heard a very strange and frightening sound, like a woman in distress. He wondered who it could be in such a deep forest, but some of his friends said it was from the Ulama bird, also known as the devil bird.

Myths exist in every country, and Sri Lanka is no exception. The legend goes that a husband, doubting his wife, killed their child, cooked the food, and served it to her. When she saw fingers in the soup, she ran into the forest and killed herself, transforming into the Ulama bird, whose screams can still be heard today.

Manimaran told me a series of stories about crows. I felt bad that we have labeled this innocent creature as "the cunning crow." It was an eye-opener for me about this intelligent little bird.

## A lesson in the importance of giving.

The crow's gift - The enduring relationship between crows and humans is not new. In Hinduism, there is a belief that offering food to a crow on the anniversary of an ancestor's passing allows the ancestor to come in the form of the crow to accept the offering. There is a heartwarming exchange between a young boy and a crows daily, the boy feeds the crows daily and the crow in return fetches a gift to show their gratitude. It's a gentle reminder to humanity, if a small little crow can reciprocate with gratitude, shouldn't we as humans. It's a touching gesture of appreciation, demonstrating the depth of connection between these intelligent creatures and humans.

*Lesson # 3:* **Express gratitude in small ways; it's not about the cost, but the love behind it.**

## Trash for treat.

In a theme park in France, it is the idea of Christophe Gaborit, the park's head falconer since 1993, to teach the crows to pick trash dropped by visitors and they get a treat in return. The crows understood the concept of trash for treat very fast and it started, though the park was already quite clean, this was an attempt to create an awareness among people about littering. This innovative approach, known as reward-based or positive reinforcement training, hinges on the principle of rewarding desired behavior with treats. By consistently offering a tasty incentive for each successful task completed, crows learn to associate the action with a positive outcome, fostering a cycle of continued engagement. While the treat may be small to the crow, the broader lesson it imparts to human observers is significant.

This simple yet impactful act offers valuable lessons for corporate managers too, highlighting the power of rewards and recognition in motivating teams.

### Thinking out of the box.

Crows exhibit remarkable problem-solving abilities, looks like they have a built-in AI within them. There are instances of chimps using heavy stones to break open nuts, but that's not possible for a crow, they aren't capable of lifting a heavy object to break them open. Like it's said, "where there is a will, there is a way", these crows have thought out of the box, to make it happen. They pick them up, drop them on the roads for vehicles to crack it open, they also strategically time their retrieval at traffic signals, which showcases their adaptability and foresight. While industries invest heavily in R&D for streamlining processes, these birds demonstrate efficiency through keen observation and clever execution.

*Lesson #4:* **Embrace open-mindedness and stay receptive to unconventional solutions, keeping eyes and ears open can lead to innovative breakthroughs.**

As my friend continued to tell stories about birds, I was reminded of the unfinished phrase he had left halfway:

"Can anyone teach a bird to fly, to migrate?" I asked him about it, and he shared another strange story.

## The school of migration.

Does it sound insane when I say that I teach swimming to a fish? Your answer may be a resounding yes, right? Similarly, your response might be the same if I were to say that someone could teach a bird to fly, or even to migrate. But it did happen.

Migration for a bird is akin to a pilgrimage for humans; they have a purpose, whether it's for weather, food sources, or breeding. Birds have followed this tradition for millions of years, passing on their values across generations. However, there has been a noticeable decline in migratory bird populations.

The Eurasian reed warbler undertakes a 7,000-kilometer journey annually between Europe and Africa, navigating the Sahara desert and soaring up to 6,000 meters for up to 30 hours without stopping.

Christian Moullec, an ornithologist with over two decades of bird study, undertook a remarkable mission. He raised a group of eight young geese, training them in the art of migration so they could continue this vital journey for generations to come. Using a specially crafted microlight aircraft, Moullec guides the geese along their migratory route, imparting crucial lessons on finding food, water, and navigating the skies.

As a filmmaker, Moullec documents this extraordinary endeavor in his documentary, 'The Secret Routes of Migratory Birds.' The documentary explores the challenges birds face during migration and teaches them strategies for overcoming obstacles. Moullec's ultimate goal is to release the geese to continue their pilgrimage independently, passing on their knowledge to successive generations.

Witnessing the bond between Moullec and his avian companions, both on the ground and in the sky, is nothing short of captivating. The film transports viewers on a breathtaking journey, offering a bird's-eye view of landscapes unfolding below: mountains, forests, castles, villages, and lakes, making for an unforgettable experience.

This one-hour documentary not only enlightened me about migratory birds reclaiming their lost instincts but also inspired a profound realization: life is meant to be lived on our own terms. You only live this life once, so live it not just the way you like, but the way you love. Whether it's embracing the wild or soaring high in the skies, the message is clear: seize the opportunity and go for it.

### *Lesson # 5:*

> *"Live life not just the way you like,*
> *but the way you love" – BE.*

### The magic of V (We).

Then he continued to talk about the 'V' we saw in the sky some time ago. The way my friend spoke about the 'V' secret was so knowledgeable and wise that it created doubt whether he was one of those birds in the V shape. Such was his depth of understanding.

At times, you may possess great strengths but may not be aware of them. Often, it is the people around you, be it a parent, teacher, or friend, who identify and bring out these strengths. A classic example is the story of the great athlete Usain Bolt. His teacher, noticing Bolt's long legs and arms, suggested he try sprinting. But Bolt was interested in basketball and football, not running. The teacher persisted and eventually uncovered the sprinter hiding inside Usain Bolt. These large-winged birds are their own gurus, guiding themselves to maximize the utility of their larger wingspan.

Manimaran asked me, 'Being an IT professional working for a major corporation, you must have attended many trainings. Which is the most important for a team?' The answer was obvious: 'team-building exercises.' Though technical and communication skills are important, working as a team is vital for success.

My friend added, 'If you are conducting a session on team building and want to refer to animals of the forest, there is no better reference than the bird kingdom, especially the large- winged ones. The 'V' in this V shape can symbolize any positive word that starts with V in the English language, whether it be Victory, Valuable, Visionary, or Vital. For this V to succeed, it is the WE that is most important.

**The Team.**

Team building and the essence of being a good team player revolve around understanding that the team's success depends full on the collective effort, every team player's contribution is vital to the collective achievement. Like every brick plays a crucial role in making a castle stand, it is every individual that makes a team succeed.

With fresh graduates annually entering the workforce, whether in established corporations or embarking on entrepreneurial ventures, grasping the essence of teamwork is paramount for organizational success. This underscores why major corporations invest in dedicated training and development teams. Success, in any endeavor, be it any sport or office enviroment, cricket, football or corporate ventures, stems from team effort. While exceptional individual performances like Indian Cricket team´s captain Kapil Dev's historic win in the 1983 Prudential World Cup innings against Zimbabwe exist, they are exceptions. Generally, success is swifter and surer as a team.

One may question the relevance of teamwork in individual-centric sports like tennis, boxing, or athletics. Yet, teamwork remains integral, whether it is a team game or an individual one. Behind every apparent solo performance lies a team supporting and enabling that individual's success.

## The unstoppable Federer.

Take Roger Federer's tennis career, for instance. While the spotlight often shines on him as a solo performer, there's a dedicated team operating behind the scenes.

➤ Coach Ivan Ljubicic, a former world No. 3 player, offers strategic guidance.

➢ Fitness trainer Pierre Paganani, who's been by Federer's side since he was 14, ensures

➢ peak physical condition.

➢ Agent Tony Godsick, the driving force behind Federer's career.

➢ Wife Mirka Federer, a former tennis player sidelined by a leg misalignment, shares in his triumphs as if they were her own.

Additionally, there are a range of support staff working tirelessly in the backstage.

Each member of this team plays a pivotal role. Their collective efforts, often unseen, are integral to Federer's success on the court. Similarly, a super hit movie may perform exceptionally well in theatres, with the spotlight on the Hero, Heroine, or Director. However, many people work tirelessly behind the scenes to make it happen.

**The Irony.**

Think about the inspiring story of a man who lost his hand in an accident but found hope through martial arts. At first, he was doubtful, but then he met a martial artist who taught him "white tiger kung fu," a style that uses only one hand. His handicap became an advantage, showing how teamwork and expertise can make a big difference. This story highlights the importance of working together rather than focusing on individual efforts or capacity. Only when both coordinated, they were able to succeed, not otherwise.

In today's corporate landscape, success depends on teamwork across industries, be it in IT, manufacturing, agriculture or any industry. While teamwork fosters innovation, it also invites differences and conflicts, necessitating skilled intervention for conflict resolution. Big Companies have their own training and development teams, to facilitate such initiatives through training sessions, highlighting the essence of effective teamwork.

Ironically, while humans require formal training on teamwork, animals inherently grasp its significance. Hearing to the V secret, I was wonderstruck to hear the great wisdom these birds possessed, how did they acquire this knowledge? Which management institute did they graduate from? Or which guru trained them on these skills? The truth I felt was, the insights of corporate lessons are rooted in teachings passed down from the wise elders of the jungle.

The simple question is, If a bird can, can´t we?

## The beauty of Berijam lake.

It was dusk when we had at last reached our first destination, it was a day long trek with lot of thrilling experiences and lessons to learn, the true practical lessons. We moved out of the jungle and we reached a deserted road, with lot of bushes on both sides of the road, since the vehicle traffic was less, the bushes were dominant. And we could see a huge, beautiful lake, it was a breath taking view. Gazing upon a lake untouched by tourists was a serene and enchanting experience. The water was still and untroubled, we could see the reflection of the mountains on the other side, it was like a huge mirror placed in the lake. There was no sound of tourists, no buildings, no shops, no boats in the lake, it was like having a romance with the lake all alone.

We lied down starring at the sky above with the tall trees that looked as if they were touching the skies, we took some rest, one of the guys lit up the stove and made tea, with a mix of ginger and cloves, it was a dance of a variety of flavor with every sip.

It was time to setup our tents while it was still bright, that was the first time I had an experience of setting up a tent, the smaller tents were for 2 people and the bigger ones were for 4. My friend Manimaran and myself took a 2 people tent. It was much more easier than I had thought, because these were easy to erect tents, when its easy, you prefer to use it. I was reminded of the wordings of Mr. G Ramprasad, who was the then Vice President of Parryware, while I worked for the Murugappa group, he introduced a phrase called "Easy To Do Business With". He used to emphasize not only for those who worked with external parties, but internally treat each and every one as a customer and supplier, when you are easy to do business with, they tend to work with you smoothly, resulting in better results.

### *Lesson # 6:* **Be "Easy To Do Business With"**

It was playtime then, it was a competition of who can throw stones that hops the maximum times and later we had some singing sessions. The usual get together in the night with friends, we end up taking about ghost stories, but this was a different group altogether, they were sharing their experiences in their adventure trips. I was the only one who was trekking for the first time, rest were used to it, as it was getting dark, the natural fear grips you, what if any animal was around, bisons were quite common in that area. My friend assured me that with the smell of people, they tend to keep away, though it was comforting, there was always that 1% of doubt in mind, but having gone all the way, you have no options but to stay, there were no houses or lodges around Berijam. I was reminded that there was no Plan B, only Plan A, some day when I start a business, I should also go with only Plan A.

Then we collected some woods, put up a small bonfire sort of setup, as the chillness was gripping us, the heat from the bonfire was comforting. They had chosen a place with not much of trees around for the bonfire, being locals brought up in the hills, they seemed quite responsible to ensure that we have to be extra careful with fire, and there was an additional tag for everyone, being animal lovers, they took extra care in every act. We sat in a circle around the fire and I reminded my friend Manimaran about the V Secret which he had promised to share when we had more time. And here it goes.

**The secret of V.**

Many of us would have noticed birds flying in a V shape in the sky, its not a random occurrence or they fly just like that, this is a pattern they follow consistently and religiously, just like the army march past. While some may know that they transmit energy to each other for a longer and smoother flight, there was much more depth to this behavior. They were such valuable lessons to me, that even incorporating a few of these techniques into our daily lives could pave the way for significant success.

✓ **The purpose.**

Birds flying in a V-shape have a purpose, most are migratory, covering short, medium, or long distances. Just like high-flying jets, those at higher altitudes are long-distance migrants. Short- distance birds move for food, medium-distance cover hundreds of miles, and long-distance fly thousands for breeding. Visiting Vedanthangal, a bird sanctuary near Chennai, I marveled at birds flocking there annually, some from as far as Australia. Despite our puzzlement, they return year after year, generation after generation, drawn by something unseen to us but vital to them. Their pilgrimage-like journey underscores their clear purpose and unwavering commitment to their chosen destination.

*Lesson #7:* **Organizations must have a clear purpose, defined mission and vision, along with a well-defined path, goals, and strategies to achieve them. Vision and mission are not only for organizations but for individuals too. Leaders bear the responsibility of steering the organization in the right direction, whether it's for profit, growth targets, or service objectives. While employees rely on the organization, it's crucial for leaders to ensure alignment with the purpose and direction. Just as every bird in a migrating flock understands its purpose, organizations must ensure that all employees grasp the mission clearly.**

**Lesson for the families – a yearly trip all the way from Australia to India is not only for the migration or breeding, but it's a like a family get together. So, ensure to save some money every month for a yearly travel. Saving is good, but experience is too good. It is the experience that will be worth carrying in your memories, rather than money.**

If bird's can, can't we?

✓ **The SOP's.**

SOPs (Standard Operating Procedures) is a familiar term in Corporates today, it's like a checklist detailing routine activities and how to execute them. Despite clear instructions, is it adhered to is a question, we always work based on what we have in our memory rather than following a checklist because we feel that we know what is written.

Imagine a tour that you plan with your family or friends, there is a lot of planning that is done, the travel, stay, food, where to visit, the costing and the list goes on and we have technology to assist us, right from split wise to share costs to itinerary, still we face some hiccups. On the contrary, these birds plan for their journey crossing thousands of miles, with no technology assistance, just by remembering what has been passed on over generations.

*Lesson # 8:* **The tragic sinking of the Titanic serves as a strong reminder of the consequences of oversight and deviation from standard procedures. Despite being hailed as unsinkable, the Titanic's** maiden voyage ended in disaster due to a series of errors. Basic SOPs, including the omission of binoculars and the captain's misjudgment regarding speed in iceberg-prone waters, were overlooked.

There is a Titanic museum in Southampton in the UK, where the Titanic started its first (and last) journey, which shows the court trails, for those crew members who had survived, in a court setup that resembles the same with voice in the back ground. Listening to it, it felt like it would have been better to have died in the Titanic rather than undergo these trials.

Follow the SOP's, because human error is inevitable, you may miss a step, it may take an extra minute to put a tick in the check list, but missing a step, can involve hours of RCA (Root Cause Analysis). Just like the Titanic, to check if the binoculars have been taken from the dock would have taken a few minutes, but saving, rather ignoring those minutes costed huge loss of lives and money.

If birds can adhere to SOPs without the aid of pen and paper, surely, we can too, with the help of computers and laptops.

If bird's can, can't we?

✓ **The Leader.**

A leader is one who guides from the front, as seen in tales like that of Alexander the Great and his horse Bucephalus, illustrating remarkable leadership qualities. We will look into the role the horse played in Alexander's life separately, we will look at the leadership qualities exhibited by these majestic long winged birds.

In the V, the bird at the forefront assumes the role of leader, drawing from ancestral knowledge of the route, including food sources and resting spots. I am reminded of the poem that was in my English lesson, by Charles Baudelaire "The Albatross," written in the 1840s, explaining the graceful presence of albatrosses alongside ships, symbolizing leadership and freedom.

*"Often, to amuse themselves, the men of a crew Catch albatrosses, those vast sea birds*

*That indolently follow a ship, as it glides over the deep, briny sea."*

The lead bird, flanked by backups on both sides, expends additional energy, setting the pace for the flock. Those trailing birds, benefit from the aerodynamic advantage provided by the preceding bird, easing their flight. In case the leading bird needs a break, its backup seamlessly assumes leadership, the last bird in the V will not even know that a change has happened at the front. The flock selects and follows the leader with faith; they ask no questions about the route or decision-making process. There is no election or voting, but the leader is followed meticulously.

*Lesson # 9:* **To select the leader for the team, once you select, follow their guidance with faith. Not all decisions may be correct, while 1 or 2 out of 10 decisions may face failure, still the majority 8 or 9**

**prove correct. Continually questioning every step will impede progress toward your destination. Trust the leadership team to steer the course. The pivotal phase lies in the decision-making process of appointing a leader.**

**A classic example - after spending 27 years in prison, Nelson Mandela's release sparked national anticipation of taking action against those responsible for his imprisonment. However, Mandela chose a different path, opting for forgiveness. His call for unity resonated with the people, who followed him without hesitation, showcasing immense respect. Mandela's authority stemmed not from coercion but from the genuine respect he earned from his people.**

**"A leader to gain respect, not demand for it." – BE**

**And have a backup to the leader, the transition should be so smooth with no vacuum created due to the change.**

If a bird can, can't we?

✓  **Communication is the key to every lock.**

Are communication skills important only in corporate settings? Absolutely not. They're essential not in just offices but in every aspect of life. Smooth internal communication is crucial for effective external communication. Within our bodies, a remarkable system of communication exists, originating in the brain or the heart sometimes. This communication occurs through the nervous system, seamlessly transmitting messages to different body parts. Nature's design within our body ensures flawless communication, enabling rapid reaction to surroundings. Imagin the swift response of your hand when it touches fire, the message is passed on from the tip of the finger through the nerves system to the brain and the brain triggers an immediate response to withdraw the hand and the hand obeys the instruction with no question. Every part of the body coordinates seamlessly, ensuring swift action to prevent harm. This synchronized communication and rapid decision-making exemplify the beauty and efficiency of the body's internal communication system.

What does the V shape have to teach to us about communication skills?

The leader of the bird flock guides from the front, positioned at the top of the V shape. This arrangement allows each bird to have a broader view. If the last bird, situated farthest from the leader, spots a ship or land in its view, it relays the information upwards. The leader then decides whether to alter the course. This parallels the bottom-up approach in organizations, where frontline workers possess valuable insights into daily challenges and can offer good suggestions for process improvement. For true progress, engaging with employees at the grassroots level is essential. Effective communication involves active listening.

**A classic example.**

The Japanese soap factory problem. Once, a Japanese consumer bought a bar of soap from a shop, only to find the box empty upon returning home. Annoyed, he returned to the shop to complain. The issue reached the company's CEO, who took it seriously. He convened his top engineers to devise a permanent solution. After much brainstorming, they proposed installing an X-ray scanning machine on the conveyor belt to detect empty packages. However, the factory operator suggested a simpler solution: placing a fan instead. Since empty soap boxes are lightweight, they would be blown away. This ingenious idea saved the company significant costs, demonstrating the value of frontline insights.

This is an example of the importance of considering simple, practical solutions over complex, expensive ones and to have an open mind to the problems and solutions. Moral of the story is to listen to every voice is the key. Similarly, the bird in the last leg, its voice will be heard and considered, no voice will go unnoticed or unheard. The flow of information from the last bird to the one at the fore-front is smooth and reaches without any distortion, though there are so many birds in between.

Humans face challenges though there is a language to communicate, these birds, exhibit remarkable communication skills with no words.

*Lesson # 10:* **"Communication is the key to every lock" If a bird can, can't we?**

✓ **Money matters**

The crux of a business to succeed lies in the efficiency of its leaders to steer it to success, to deliver quality products, to maximize profits, explore various avenues to generate revenue, cost reduction strategies, negotiation with suppliers, improved logistics, reduced cycle time, reduce wastage, automation, introduction of AI, etc.

These birds flying in V formation offer valuable insights into energy efficiency, while the intricacies of aerodynamics remain a mystery, the V shape proves instrumental in conserving energy. The synchronized flapping of their expansive wings propels air in a direction that benefits subsequent birds, allowing them to effortlessly glide on the upward currents generated. Though the leader has to put in the extra effort, the collective energy transfer enables the flock to fly with ease. So is the expectation in a leader.

*Lesson # 11:* **"put maximum effort as a leader to minimize the effort for the team" - BE If birds can, can´t we?**

✓ **The backup**

In software projects, change management place a very crucial role, there will be a weekly or a monthly CAB (Change Advisory Board) call, in which all changes moving to production will be discussed, though the CAB is expected to play a very critical role in the smooth movement of the changes, my observation has been that the CAB manager is a person who is neither technical nor functional, in most cases, have seen them focus on areas they are comfortable with which are not really critical to the change. The person driving the CAB should be techno-functional or should be supported by a techno-functional consultant, ask relevant questions that are critical to the movement, about the impact, backup plan, test results, about performance, etc.

A backup plan being crucial to any change that is moved to production environment, on the contrary, if you are starting a business, is a backup plan important, the immediate answer may look like an "Yes", though in my view, I would say that you should start a business with no Plan B. There should be only one plan, which it to make it happen. But, it is important to have a backup for every role. The bird right in the front leads, if it needs rest, the second line steps up and takes over, the transition is so smooth that the birds down the line, do not know that a change has happened at the top. In the event of the leader's absence, whether due to illness or any other reason, the business must continue to function seamlessly, as its employees and stakeholders rely on its continuity.

**A classic example.**

The empire built by Dhirubhai Ambani, Reliance Industries, stood as a pillar of support for countless employees and stakeholders. Recognizing the importance of continuity, Dhirubhai meticulously groomed his sons to seamlessly step into leadership roles in his absence. Their capable stewardship not only sustained the business but propelled its growth exponentially. This ensured uninterrupted service for employees, suppliers, and customers alike, safeguarding against disruption in the event of a leader's absence.

### Lesson # 12: "A lesson for organizations to cultivate a capable second line" If birds can, can't we?

#### ✓ Being in sync

These birds operate in perfect harmony, driven by a shared goal of reaching a specific destination. Each bird understands the importance of teamwork, to be in sync, refusing to let their companions down at all times, knowing that collective effort makes the task easier for everyone. If a bird falls out of sync, it immediately senses the increased strain on its wings, readjusting to align with the team and maintain energy flow. They remain attuned to the team at all times.

In the corporate world, we often lose synchronization with other teams or within our own, driven by factors like ego, misunderstanding, or miscommunication, unaware of the ripple effects. Success becomes attainable only when we work together seamlessly, prioritizing the common goal over individual interests.

#### Lessons learnt.

With these birds, to be in sync, this process occurs seamlessly, without any need for manual intervention or directives from a leader. Even though the leader may not be aware of these adjustments, the birds take initiative without waiting for external guidance.

Similarly, in organizational teamwork, it's our individual responsibility to realign ourselves when we're out of sync, without waiting for explicit instructions. Birds know that the journey is long and to be in sync is crucial to attaining the target, there is no place for ego in their structure.

If a bird can, can´t we?

### ✓ The art of delegation

When the leading bird grows weary, they seamlessly hand over the reins to the second bird, ensuring a smooth transition with no gaps. This flawless delegation is vital for the team's success; they understand that any disruption in the handover process could lead to failure. Instead of bearing the entire burden themselves, they master the art of delegation, empowering the second line to take charge while they step back.

In organizations, the sudden absence of a team member due to illness, leave, or resignation can create a significant gap. This occurs when vital details are hoarded and not shared or documented, leading to a reliance on individual contributors. However, true success is

achieved when the departure of an employee causes no disruption to the workflow. This indicates that the departing employee has effectively developed and empowered the second line or trained their team adequately.

### Lessons learnt.

Delegate tasks to your team, develop your team, remember, delegate the work, not the responsibility.

✓ **Acceleration & Visibility**

The V shape adopted by birds serves two essential purposes: acceleration and improved visibility. This configuration enables them to reach their destination swiftly while also enhancing their awareness of surrounding opportunities and threats. Similarly, in the corporate world, the primary objective is often rapid profit generation, necessitating both strong leadership drive and keen market insight into opportunities and competition.

**Lessons learnt.**

The leader, not only the top most, but there are leader in every level, each and every leader to look at how to accelerate performance and also keep their eyes and ears open, keep a watch on opportunities and threats.

If a bird can, can´t we?

✓ **Collaboration and empowerment**

Each bird in the V-shaped formation collaborates seamlessly, empowering one another and collectively working towards their common goal. They contribute to the team's growth by making tasks easier for their counterparts.

Similarly, it is important to identify the strength of each member and build the team accordingly, the essence lies in the reciprocal flow of energy, making teamwork smoother, and in listening to feedback from all levels, ensuring mutual understanding and action.

**Lessons learnt.**

From these beautiful and intelligent creatures, we can glean the art of both top-down and bottom-up approaches. Learning to collaborate and empower others toward a common goal is essential.

If a bird can, can't we?

✓ **Trust and support**

Trust is paramount among these migratory birds. Each bird in the formation places its trust in the leader, believing they're being guided in the right direction. This trust extends seamlessly down the line, with each bird relying on the one ahead. If a bird momentarily falls out of sync, there's no panic; they quickly realign, trusting their fellow birds to understand.

In contrast, humans often lack this patience and trust. In teams, mistakes are quickly highlighted rather than forgiven. Similarly, on the road, we honk impatiently at delays instead of waiting patiently.

Support is another crucial aspect. If a bird falls ill or struggles to keep pace, it drops out of formation. Yet, it's not abandoned; fellow birds accompany it until it recovers or they reunite with the flock. This unwavering support ensures the journey continues smoothly for all.

**Lessons learnt.**

In a team, trust is the cornerstone of success. We must believe in our leader's guidance and support one another, both professionally and personally. If a team member faces difficulties, extend a helping hand. By fostering trust and offering support, we ensure a smooth journey for the entire team.

If a bird can, can't we?

✓ **Appreciate**

Birds employ various sounds and gestures to express different behaviors, such as mating, signaling threats, expressing gratitude, and they have a sound to appreciate too, for the presence and contribution of the bird in the V shape.

In organizations too, recognition plays a vital role in motivating employees. While top executives may not always offer direct praise, it's crucial for immediate supervisors to acknowledge and appreciate their team members achievements. It is said that employees often leave not companies but their bosses. Adopting the principle of "praise in public and chide in

person" fosters a positive team environment and enhances overall performance. Celebrate successes openly and address mistakes privately to encourage continuous improvement.

**Lessons learnt.**

Learn to appreciate even the smallest acts worthy of recognition; often, it costs nothing but a few words of appreciation or a brief email to a higher-level manager. A simple smile and greeting as you walk around the office can make a significant difference, brightening both your day and those around you.

Celebrate success, not just major milestones, but also smaller achievements along the way. Recognizing these smaller victories acts as a morale booster for the team, keeping motivation levels high. Remember to recognize and reward team members for their efforts; acknowledgment goes a long way in fostering a positive work environment and encouraging continued excellence.

If birds can, can't we?

### ✓ Strategy and values

It's essential to imbibe everything you do with value and purpose, backed by a well-defined strategy. These birds adhere to a specific flying pattern, the V shape, and stick to a traditional migration route passed down through generations. Despite facing numerous challenges along the way, such as adverse weather conditions, scarcity of resources, and the need for resting spots, they remain steadfast in their migration. This commitment stems from the deep-seated belief and value instilled by their ancestors, a tradition they uphold without hesitation.

### Lessons learnt.

Organizations must establish enduring values and beliefs that resonate with future generations, inspiring them to uphold these principles as tradition, regardless of the challenges they may encounter. Having a robust strategy in place guides teams through tough decisions. It's crucial to empower teams to think innovatively and adapt to evolving circumstances, recognizing that today's challenges differ from those encountered during migrations centuries ago, the newer generation of birds adapt and evolve.

If birds can, can´t we?

## ✓ Team building

Team-building lessons are in abundance in the animal kingdom, there is no place for ego or selfishness with the common goal in mind. While they lack business schools or engineering colleges, animals excel in communication, teamwork, and leadership with no formal education or certificate. Without textbooks or PowerPoint presentations, they teach us valuable life lessons simply through observation. It's not about what they say, but rather what we can learn by listening and observing their natural behaviors.

Today, let's embark on our maiden flight, much like the bird taking its first leap from the nest. Let's venture out, embrace challenges, soar to new heights, and immerse ourselves in the captivating symphony of wings. Remember that there may be a descent, but if a small and simple bird can fight to ascend again, shouldn´t we? We can.

The lessons around the bonfire were numerous, one set of people prepared dinner by the side, it was the simple 2 minute noodles, though very simple, it had an extra flavor because that was the only food available to us for many kilometers around. The time was almost 11.00pm and we decided to sleep, it was cold, we got into our tents, into our sleeping bags, pulled up the zip and it looked like we were Egyptian mummies. With the tiredness of the trek, I was asleep within minutes, sleep has always arrived within minutes for me, at times, I would fall asleep during the descent itself.

The time was around 06.00am, the Sun was slowly painting the sky with a lighter coting, over the dark shades, we woke up the next day morning with the sound of birds, the natural alarms. Another round of fresh tea, we refreshed ourselves, had bread and eggs for breakfast and we continued our journey.

If the first day was a scary trek inside the forest area, the second day was a different scary experience. We reached the hilltop, and it had a beautiful view of a valley in front of us and a scary waterfall, there was a small structure that looked like a prayer spot, with a sickle inside the structure, all my friends knelt and prayed for a minute, I did too. Then, one of them explained that they have been trekking along this path for quite long and the ones with whom they started, used to spend a minute here to pray, but they did not know the significance of the spot. It reminded me of the birds following their ancestors' path as passed on over generations.

It looked like the end of the range of mountains, there was no more area to trek forward and I was confused which way next or is it that they visited that place only for the prayer time. And to my surprise, they started walking further near the waterfall and we had to literally hold the weeds by the side of the water, place our legs carefully on the gaps on the gaps between the rocks, not to slip. The soft winds carried the water that was flowing to us like a drizzle from the side. The water flow was quite normal, it

97

wasn't heavy. At the 3rd waterfall point, we took a break, we could slide down along with the water to land in a pool of water, it was like a natural water park. We had a good time playing in water for half an hour and in between my friends offered me their binoculars, showing me some of the native birds in the surroundings, they were explaining about the specialty of its color, the tail, the beaks, looked like they were in a romance with the birds. We continued our journey, finally when we reached a flat surface, I turned and looked at the path we had come and there were 5 waterfalls that we had crossed along, it looked terribly scary. Then it was a walk in flat surface for quite some time, then an uphill trek and we reached Mannavanur, there was a small hotel, where we had our lunch, it was a delicious lunch, not sure if it was delicious because we did not have proper food for 2 days or if it was really delicious, but it was a good meal. There was a van waiting for us to take us back to Kodai and I had slept in the van, to wake up only at Kodai.

## Conclusion

When a bird is tired flying, decides to rest on a branch, it does no evaluation of a branch, whether it is strong enough to support its weight, because of the confidence it has on its own strength. If the branch breaks, it knows that it will not fall down, it knows that its wings are strong enough to take flight. Similarly, we humans also possess an inherent resilience to weather any storm. Life's setbacks shouldn't signal the end; they're merely detours on our journey. Tragically, we often hear of young lives cut short by exam failures, business losses or breakups.

Even those who failed to board the Titanic are not failures, they are actually lucky, similar can be your situation, though it may look like you have failed today, it may be for tomorrow´s good. The vastness of the world offers countless avenues for survival and success. The key is to trust in our ability to persevere and forge ahead.

Ask the simple question, if a bird can, can´t we? And you will move on when faced with challenges.


*- Be Happy Always -*

♦

# Be (E) Aware of The Bee

"honey & sting are from the same bees
honey is sweet & stings are painful
so, are our words" - BE

## The walking routine

We all know that walking has a lot of benefits, let it be betterment of health, keeping fit, active and so on, apart from these known benefits, I had a bonus benefit, it was the introduction to an old man called Charles, who was a beekeeper in Geneva. I never missed my walking routine as the place was so beautiful that my wife and myself would never miss to take advantage of it. On our path, we have noticed an old traditional wooden house that resembled the cuckoo clocks, we often heard a strange buzzing sound when we passed by this house.

One fine day, during our usual walk, we saw an old man standing outside the house. Since we didn't look like locals, we would just smile and greet each other with a "bonjour," meaning good day. This continued for days, eventually leading to short conversations. I asked him if there was a beehive in his garden because of the buzzing sound we always heard. He told me he was a beekeeper, which was a new concept for us then. We had only seen bees in hives at temples or mountain ranges and had heard of people keeping dogs or cats, but not bees.

He invited us for coffee and to see how he keeps the bees in his backyard, we were seated in the receiving hall of the traditional Swiss house, there were lot of old photograph of their family on one side of the wall, it was so beautiful, Charles said that it helps to recall the memories of those loved ones, once in a while. We have always heard people say not to think about the past but about the present and future, but at times, to recall and cherish those wonderful days is a lovely experience. He was preparing the coffee and the air carried the aroma of the coffee from the kitchen to the hall, it created an expectation for us to wait for the coffee to arrive, as conveyed by the aroma, the coffee was a rejuvenation experience.

Charles took us through his long life of 70 years in a quick 7 minute conversation, retired from the army, moved back to his ancestral home when his wife passed away, children were settled in different places, he said he has visited India and Tibet while he was young, stayed for some time in the monasteries in the Himalayan region and has read Indian literature and learnt Sanskrit as well. Sounded strange for a Swiss to have interest on monasteries and Sanskrit. He started bee keeping as a hobby influenced by reading the story of accidental bee keepers. It increased my curiosity to ask about the accidental beekeepers.

## Beekeepers by accident

Marianne and Matt Gee, the founders of Gees Bees Honey Company in Canada, became beekeepers unexpectedly in 2009 when they discovered a colony of honeybees in the wall of their new home. Instead of taking help from professionals who can help to get rid of them, they chose to rescue and care for the bees, they took professional help to safely relocate the hive. Witnessing the delicate process of hive relocation left them awestruck. Simply by identifying and relocating the queen bee, the entire colony followed suit, demonstrating the mesmerizing dance of nature's monarch: the queen bee. This ignited their passion for beekeeping and ended up crafting exceptional honey. They said that it brought immense joy in knowing that they sweeting the day for many with their pure, all-natural honey.

Reading this, Charles took up beekeeping as a hobby, initially started with distributing the honey to family and friends, ended up falling in love with the bees and the feedback from the receivers, he increased the capacity of bees and now selling it to the local markets as well.

He took us through his journey of how he fell in love with the bees, he asked a question for which I did not have an answer at that time for sure, it was - what can we learn from an insect weighing just 0.1 to 0.2 grams and measuring between 2 to 39 mm in length, when we as humans average 70 to 80 kilos and stand 5 to 6 feet tall? The scale seems entirely disproportionate. Yet don't underestimate the bum(hum)ble bee. Despite a brain the size of a pinhead, it possesses remarkable abilities. This tiny creature can recognize landmarks and memorize nectar and pollen sources for over a week.

There's a wealth of wisdom to grasp from these tiny insects. They excel in mathematics, architecture, and even warehouse management. Their communication skills are exemplary, offering valuable lessons for the corporate world. Indeed, these tiny creatures showcase greatness in various aspects. I was surprised to hear that they are good mathematics, architecture and warehouse management, you can imaging the size of their brain in proportion to their body size, it may be hardly the size of a pin head, where is mathematics and architectural excellence in this tiny brain coming from.

The way he took us through, I was fascinated by the beekeeper, rather by the bees, found myself captivated by these creatures as we heart only a fraction of their capacity. He said that not all bees are honey producers, but the beekeepers take the center stage by nurturing them in hives for honey production and vital pollination services. This interdependence between plants and bees is profound, bees seek nectar from flowers to sustain their hives, while flowers rely on bees for pollination, forming an indispensable relationship.

He asked me about the size and shape of the pears around that area, I recalled my walking path and I nodded my head, saying yes, they looked beautiful, he further questioned if I had noticed the size and shape, to which I couldn't recall. He said that bees play a role in flavor, taste and shape of the fruits, with the natural pollination caused by bees. There are others ways through which pollination happens, like wind and water, but bees are the primary agents. In some parts of China, where bees have vanished totally, manual pollination happens with sticks and brushes, consequently, the fruits yielded from such efforts are not only less flavorful but also possess irregular shapes, highlighting the crucial role bees play in maintaining ecosystem balance and agricultural productivity. Studies have been carried out on this and proved to be correct.

He said that a portion of your prayer to God thanking him for the food in your table daily, a percentage of it should go to the bees, it's astonishing to realize the profound connection between our meals and these tiny beings. One third of the food supply hinges due to the pollination caused by bees.

Small in size but quantifying their contribution to our world is a daunting task, perhaps even beyond comprehension. If we were to assign an industrial value to the services provided by the animal kingdom, it would undoubtedly reach into a multibillion-dollar range. Yet, the irony lies in the fact that bees offer their services freely. For humans, anything without a price tag often goes unappreciated. Consider the air we breathe; it's freely available, and thus often taken for granted. It's only when faced with a hospital bill for an oxygen cylinder that we realize its true worth. Unfortunately, such realizations often come too late.

In nature, from the largest animals like elephants to the tiniest like bees, each plays a vital role in maintaining ecosystems. They collaborate seamlessly without expecting anything in return. Despite our awareness of such principles from ancient teachings, our actions often fall short. It's like possessing knowledge without wisdom.

We had our coffee and we stepped out into the back yard, it was a huge space and there were lot of wooden boxes on one side, 3 boxes one on top of the other. He had a kit to handle the bees, he said that he used all of those initially, but now having got used to them, he only uses the face mask which is like a net covering the face. He pulled out one layer from the top box which had a sort of net with lot of bees on it and it had a deposit of honey, he went to explain that the queen bee lives at the bottom most box, laying eggs, there is a layer to protect it from moving upward to the box above, then the worker bees and drones. Bees like many other animals operate within a matriarchal society. The queen lays thousands of eggs in its life span of 2 to 3 years. Drones, or male bees, have a singular purpose: mating. Remarkably, once a drone successfully mates, it dies. Failure in this endeavor results in expulsion from the colony, leading to death due to exposure to the weather outside the hive. Drones typically have a short life span. In a comical sense, the main job of a male bee, or drone, is to mate and then, well, that's pretty much the end of life for them. The female worker bees are the real champions, who work tirelessly for the wellbeing of the colony, with a short life span of 4 to 6 weeks.

While explaining how the setup works, Charles went to say something in Sanskrit, I was taken aback, made me feel bad that I myself could not repeat it, but he was so fluent, apart from being fluent, I was surprised that he could remember it so well and also to go to explain what it meant.

It is something like, you will have lot of tourist and visitors visiting the Taj Mahal to see it from all over the world, but the locals living in Agra would have not visited, it is normal to ignore the importance if you are too close to it. Same was the case here.

**Bhagavad Gita, Chapter 2, Verse 47 says:**

कर्मण्येवाधिकारस्ते रू फलेषु कदाचन।

रू कर्मफलहेतुर्भमर ॑ाम ते सङ्गोऽस्त्वकर्मधि॥ २-४७

*"You have the right to work only but never to its fruits"*

He also went to explain the crux of this sloka - the saying finds its perfect embodiment in these female worker bees. Despite their short lifespan of 4 to 6 weeks, they tirelessly collect honey and store it in the hive. Their diligent efforts serve to safeguard the hive during winter, ensuring its warmth even though they won't be alive to benefit from it. Yet, they persist in their duties with unwavering dedication.

Worker bees undertake a multitude of tasks during their short lives, from housekeeping duties to policing the hive, foraging for food, caring for the young, regulating temperature, and even exploring for new hives if necessary. They are true multitaskers, constantly on the fast track for promotion within the hive.

Remarkably, a female worker bee weighs just one-tenth of a gram, yet she can carry back nectar weighing half her own weight, sometimes even more. To gather a kilogram of nectar, a bee must embark on an astounding 50,000 trips, or it would require the collective effort of 50,000 bees to make just one trip.

Consider this: a bee can make twenty trips a day over a one-kilometer round trip, bringing back 0.4 grams of nectar each time. Therefore, harvesting 1 kilogram of nectar requires journeys totaling more than 40,000 kilometers, equivalent to the circumference of the Earth.

It's truly mind-boggling to contemplate the capabilities of these tiny creatures, all done without any expectation of reward.

Indeed, many of nature's creations operate on a similar principle, they give tirelessly, perhaps seeking nothing in return except, perhaps, love.

## The wild honey

He said that although we raise bees at home and gather honey that is quite pure, the taste of wild honey is undeniably beyond comparison. People risk their lives in the mountain cliffs to extract wild honey. It is said that honey extraction has been there for period as old as 15,000 years ago, the cave paintings in Valencia in Spain prove this and the ones in India show case scenes of honey gathering, dating back to 15,000 to 11,000 BC.

I was surprised with his knowledge of the bees, it showed that he was not growing bees just as a hobby but as a passion, else you would not want to know so much about them, unless you fall in love with them. He was one for sure, he asked another strange question.

## The unbelievable shelf life.

How long do you think honey can last on the shelf? Give it your best guess, and let's see if you're close to the actual answer. You think it over as well and then read on.

In 1922, archaeologists exploring King Tut's tomb stumbled upon jars of honey dating back over 3,000 years, yet it was still perfectly edible. Honey has long been revered as "liquid gold" in ancient Egypt, used not only in baking and brewing but also medicinally, with Cleopatra even indulging in honey baths for beauty. The ancient Egyptians were pioneers in beekeeping, harnessing bee products for various purposes, including mummification. Even older honey, over 5,500 years old, was found in Georgia in 2003, surpassing the age of the Egyptian discovery by two millennia. Despite its remarkable age, honey remains edible, leaving us wondering about the secret behind its enduring freshness.

## The Dancing Queen.

We got back to inside the home and I could hear the song "Dancing Queen" from the old and famous ABBA album and Charles said that he purchased the dancing queen initially with some worker bees. We know the power of the queen in the game of chess; she is more powerful than the king. If the queen is lost, half the game is lost. So are the queens in the world of bees, you will be surprised to hear that once the queen dies, the colony of bees with an average of 20 to 80 thousand bees is dismantled totally. When hive overpopulation occurs, worker bees embark on scouting missions to find a suitable location for a new hive. Upon discovery, they return and convey their findings through a unique dance, signaling their fellow bees about the promising site. Upon confirmation, a new queen is nurtured with royal jelly and pollen. Once matured, she leads a portion of the colony to establish a new home.

Then he switched topic from the dancing queen to the lost queen, went on to ask us to picture the chaos if the Queen of the United Kingdom were suddenly missing from the

Royal Palace, it would be a total chaos. I was reminded of the old movie "Roman Holiday" in the 1970´s where the queen goes missing while on a trip to Italy, though it was a romantic comedy by Gregory Peck and Audrey Hepburn, in reality it would be a lot different.

**The Lost Queen.**

It so happened for this Queen, a remarkable incident unfolded when a swarm of 20,000 bees relentlessly pursued a car for two days, driven by their determination to rescue their trapped queen. A bee expert called to assess the situation discovered the queen confined within the car's trunk, causing the rest of the colony to linger outside. Once freed, the queen led her devoted subjects away, ending the extraordinary chase.

According to CNN, the unexpected ordeal occurred to Carol Howarth, an elderly woman, following a visit to a nature reserve in Wales. Unaware of the royal passenger she had unwittingly transported, Carol was taken aback when thousands of bees descended upon her car as she stopped for shopping in Haverfordwest. The persistent swarm, having tracked her vehicle from the reserve, steadfastly clung to the car's rear for over 48 hours.

It was almost 09.00pm in the night, the sky was becoming darker, it was almost 2 hours we had spent with Charles and his bees, we bid adieu to Charles, it was a new friendship we had gained due to our walking practice and I got to know a lot more about bees talking to this new but old friend of mine.

**The unsung heroes.**

It became a sub-routine to have a coffee and a chat, within the main routine of walking, the next day was a weekend, so we got to spend some extra time with the beekeeper. He said that these tiny creatures are carrying so much weight on their shoulders, they are the unsung heroes of this world. As usual, he asked us a question and as usual we had no answer to it, we did not have google on those days, to immediately use the search engine.

"Do you know how many stomach does a bee have?", with the question I knew it was definitely more than 1, else this question would not come and with the size of a bee, there cannot be many, so my guess was two and it was right. Though my answer was right, I really was wondering how could or why would a bee need two stomachs. One stomach is reserved for their own sustenance, while the other serves as a vessel for transporting nectar back to the hive. This nectar not only feeds their fellow colony members but also contributes to the construction and insulation of the hive, ensuring warmth during harsh winters.

Another astounding aspect of bee's social responsibility is their capacity to collect a very tiny amounts of honey throughout their lifetime. While individually negligible, this honey collectively sustains the hive during winter months. Every drop they gather is crucial, like how we say that every single drop makes an ocean. Their relentless dedication to this task aims to safeguard the hive and ultimately, the queen residing within it. What's truly remarkable is that the worker bees, tirelessly foraging for food, won't live to witness the fruits of their labor. They selflessly contribute to the hive's survival, ensuring its continuation even at the cost of their own lives.

I couldn´t say no, had to agree, yes, in essence, bees are the unsung heroes.

### Ants and bees, the cousins.

Charles said that there are lot of similarities between ants and bees, almost as if bees were ants with wings, and ants were bees without wings. Despite their differences, these tiny creatures share remarkable similarities.

Both exhibit extraordinary architectural prowess, worthy of admiration from the most seasoned architects. Their construction of intricate homes is a marvel, meticulously designed to withstand weather extremes, shield against winter's chill, and repel intruders from rival colonies. Within these intricate structures lie specialized chambers, each serving distinct purposes: chamber for the queen, for food storage and accommodations for drones and workers. Both of these species boasts of no formal degree, yet their architectural prowess is beyond imagination.

In some species, both ants and bees possess dual stomachs, it's a social responsibility that they posess. One for personal sustenance, while the other serves as a vessel for transporting food back to the hive or anthill.

Both the worker castes of ants and bees selflessly dedicate their lives to the greater good of their species, despite not living long enough to enjoy the fruits of their labor. The roles of males in both species follow a similar trajectory, they mate with the queen and then perish, it's a tragicomedy.

## Move as millions, survive as one.

'Move as millions, survive as one' may ring true for some migrations, like the awe-inspiring wildebeest migration in Africa, but the same cannot be said for bees, whose migrations are often coerced.

Historically, we've heard tales of people forcibly transported across continents for labor, we all know the plight of slaves. Today, while voluntary migration for work is common, driven by opportunity or fascination, like the maximum migrations were due to the Information Technology industry. Bees do not migrate on their own, but they are forced to, for agricultural purposes. Bees are shipped in containers from one continent to another, particularly for pollinating almond crops in Canada. This practice, driven by human self-interest, aims to boost almond yields across vast expanses of land. However, it poses significant challenges for the bees, as they struggle to adapt and sustain themselves once the pollination season ends. Unlike heir wild counterparts, these bees have no opportunity to collect honey for sustenance.

Pesticides and parasites further threaten the bees' survival, contributing to the spread of diseases within colonies. In the short lifespan of a worker bee, foraging for food is among the most arduous tasks, fraught with risks such as predation by birds and vulnerability to harsh weather conditions. It takes 12 bees their entire lifetime to make just one teaspoon of honey. To produce just one kilogram of honey, a worker bee must visit an astonishing 4 to 7 million flowers (depending on the species) within a radius of about 4 kilometers from the hive. So, think before you waste even a drop of honey, considering the immense effort of countless bees over their lifetimes.

**Booze from bees.**

Local bees contribute to the production of various alcoholic beverages by providing honey, a magical ingredient that enhances the taste of whisky, vodka, gin, or wine, imparting a unique and delightful flavor. It is an irony that this sweet produce adds taste to the flavor of liquor.

It became a routine for me to visit Charles and spend time talking about various topics and I had the opportunity to do a little bit of bee keeping wearing the net mask and extracting honey, along with my old friend. I have put together some of the conversations I have had with him, that were real time lessons for me.

The simple question was, "if a bee can, can't we?".

**The lessons from the B(ee) level management institutes.**

What I understood from my experience of beekeeping, they are tiny but have big lessons to teach humankind.

✓ **One Goal.**

The entire bee colony shares one single goal, protecting the queen and ensuring the hive's survival. With up to 80,000 bees, each bee plays a vital role in this mission, even those who won't be alive until winter, to reap the benefits of their work. Remarkably, they operate without hierarchical instructions, yet seamlessly work together toward this common objective. This efficient teamwork poses a mystery in organizational structure. Perhaps it's time for human organizations to study the organization structure of the bees, adopt similar strategies

for smoother task execution. If scent trails suffice for bee communication, why not explore analogous methods for human collaboration?

I have never seen such clear vision in any company, assume a bee hive as an organization with 80,000 workers, can you imagine that there will be a vision, a single goal, towards which all the workers will contribute selflessly with no ego, no misunderstandings, no communication gaps. In a bee hive, every single employee of the 80,000 lot work tirelessly to reach the single goal.

If bees can, can't we?

### ✓ The community dances.

Can bees dance? Absolutely. Just like humans, bees use dance as a form of communication. When a bee discovers nectar, it doesn't just keep it a secret, it dances! These tiny choreographers perform 'round dances' and

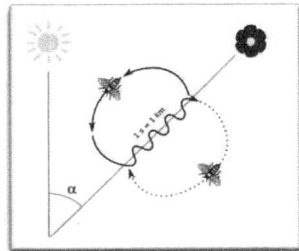

'waggle dances' to convey crucial information to their hive mates. The 'round dance' signals nearby pollen, while the intricate 'waggle dance' provides precise directions to the food source, including distance and direction, guiding fellow bees to the sweet treasure.

The dancing queen never dances, yet she orchestrates the hive's activities, directing a workforce of up to 80,000 workers. It's a fascinating realm, worthy of deeper exploration. If bees can, can't we?

### ✓ Delegate work not responsibility.

Today, we see training sessions organized on leadership and management, for those are already managers, in order to improve on their level of capacities. Effective leadership skills depends on the capacity on division and delegation of the work, to delegate work not the responsibility. Imagine a bee hive where the day to day activities happen seamlessly, to attend to the queen, to cater to the eggs and young ones, to maintain the cleanliness, to maintain the temperature within the hive, foraging for food and policing, all tasks are delegated, no supervision or monitoring is required. There is no moon-lighting like what we have seen in the IT companies post covid season, no bee lives in one hive and works for another. All of these instructions are given by the one queen in the hive.

If bees can, can't we?

### ✓ Cleanliness is next to godliness.

A beehive stands as one of nature's most best preserved environments, meticulously maintained by the worker bees to keep the hive clean and to ward off disease. Every cell undergoes thorough cleaning before being repurposed for honey storage or housing new eggs.

Reflecting on my experience at TVS Group, I recall being tasked with the care of a machine on the factory floor, despite my background in Information Technology. Initially, I approached the responsibility half-heartedly. However, as time passed, a sense of attachment grew, it was like nurturing my own "baby". Gradually, routine tasks evolved into cherished habits, with each cleaning session feeling like a vital ritual for the machine's well-being. If there was a day where the machine stopped working for any reason, it made me feel sad as well.

This sense of responsibility extends to my daily routine, where I now make it a habit to clean my laptop before diving into work. What began as a task has transformed into a ritual of care and commitment.

If bees can, can´t we?

### ✓ The guardians of the society.

Once a bee is capable of stinging, it qualifies to become a guardian of the hive. These "policemen" position themselves at the hive entrance, instinctively protecting it from intruders. This transition occurs seamlessly, without any formal ceremony, bees simply assume their roles and carry out their duties, without being told to do so.

It's high time for humans to learn lessons from these tiny creatures and embrace our social responsibility as guardians of our society. The most simple of all, just as you don't need a policeman at every traffic signal to enforce stopping at a red light, innate instincts can guide us toward fulfilling our roles as stewards of our communities.

If bees can, can't we?

### ✓ They are great mathematicians.

Bees exhibit remarkable mathematical prowess, evidenced by their construction of hexagonal beehive cells. Research indicates that this shape maximizes honey storage efficiency, minimizing wasted space compared to circles, squares, or triangles. Remarkably, bees haven't pursued formal degrees in mathematics, they know not algebra, trigonometry or differential calculus, but they know what they need, they possess an innate understanding of optimization and resource utilization, relying on instinct to create highly efficient structures. There's much to learn from their approach, especially for those involved in warehouse management. If a bee with the brain size of tiny pin head, can think so much and shape their bee hive for an optimal storage, shouldn't we as humans, but we humans need a degree and a formal training session.

If bees can, can't we?

### ✓ Unity is strength.

The phrase "easier said than done" holds true, while we recognize the benefits of unity, can we truly achieve it?. Yet, bees, much like ants, understand the power of solidarity. Despite each bee's ability to collect only a tiny amount of nectar, they persist in their efforts, instinctively contributing to the collective well-being of the hive. How they calculate and coordinate this collective effort remains a mystery. Meanwhile, humans face similar challenges not only in workplaces but also in households, with joint families increasingly becoming nuclear units over time.

If bees can, can't we?

✓ **The alphabet V is more important than I.**

We saw that these remarkable creatures are inherently equipped with two stomachs. One for their own sustenance, while the other is dedicated to transporting nectar back to the hive. Such selflessness in such small beings is truly remarkable. In contrast, we humans often prioritize the 'I' over the 'we' displaying selfish tendencies. Bees, however, embody the essence of unity, always prioritizing the collective 'we' over individual interests.

If bees can, can't we?

✓ **No annual appraisals.**

Without yearly objectives, appraisal cycles, or annual increases, bees continue their work with unwavering passion. Essentially, they highlight the concept of pursuing one's passion, working on what you love means you're not working even for a single day. Bees intuitively recognize their strengths and assign themselves tasks accordingly, whether it's foraging, hive maintenance, or guarding. They approach their responsibilities with unwavering dedication.

Moreover, bees adapt to their surroundings, with different species inhabiting various landscapes. Smaller bees, for instance, tend to frequent smaller plants, such as medicinal herbs like the basil plant. Their expertise varies based on their size and environment.

Remarkably, there's no need for managerial oversight in the world of bees, they organize and execute tasks independently.

If bees can, can´t we?

### ✓ The logistics experts.

Bees excel in logistics, embarking on journeys up to 4 kilometers from their hive in search of nectar. Despite taking varied routes, they always find the shortest path back to the hive. They leave a scent trail along the way, guiding their fellow bees to the food source.

In today's corporate landscape, businesses strive to optimize last-mile delivery, reduce cycle times on delivery for both raw materials and end product, all involving significant planning and costs. In contrast, bees achieve these feats effortlessly by simply leaving scent trails. This natural communication method ensures swift and efficient collaboration among hive members, resulting in superior outcomes.

It's high time for humanity to learn from bees similar to the ingenious scent communication methods. There are invaluable lessons here for corporate logistics departments seeking to enhance efficiency, bees do these traits at zero cost.

If bees can, can't we?

## ✓ Architect cum civil engineers under one roof.

Take a moment to observe the construction of a beehive: it's a marvel of design, featuring separate chambers meticulously crafted for the queen, storage, and worker bees. Engineered to withstand various weather conditions, from rain to heat, the hive is ingeniously built with space-saving hexagonal cells for storage. Bees, in essence, embody a fusion of highly skilled civil engineers and architects.

Considering their wealth of knowledge, dexterity, and strategic planning abilities, one can't help but wonder: Could we, with all our resources and capacities, construct a home with such precision and efficiency? We will need a builder, an architect, civil engineer & workers to be deployed.

If bees can, can't we?

## ✓ Be valuable.

In today's corporate world, opportunities are plenty, but so are risks. Gone are the days of job security; one can be hired one day and let go the next if they haven't proven their value. Those who lack technical prowess or expertise are most vulnerable to sudden job loss.

Similarly, in a bee colony of up to 80,000 individuals, only a few hundred are drones, whose sole purpose is mating, they contribute nothing to the hive's productivity. When resources are scarce, drones are the first to be expelled, left to perish in the cold. The lesson is clear: To secure your place, you must demonstrate your value. Moral of the story is to be valuable, just sitting, doing nothing will work at times, not always.

Today, if all bees were to disappear, the human species would follow suit within four years. Such is the indispensable role of bees in our food chain: no bees, no food for humans. They add value, be valuable in whatever you do.

If bees can, can't we?

✓ **The succession.**

When bees detect signs of their queen's decline, whether due to injury, illness, or age, they take proactive measures to ensure the colony's continuity. They select a young larva, nurture her with royal jelly and pollen, and encase her in a protective supersedure cell. Upon emergence, this new queen assumes leadership, replacing her predecessor. Remarkably, bees navigate this succession process seamlessly, without conflict. Unlike worker bees, queens possess reproductive capabilities, a critical distinction. Upon emergence, the first queen dispatches potential rivals by stinging them, establishing her sole authority. In the rare event of dual emergence, there is a fierce battle between the two and the victorious gains the throne.

This innate ability to ensure orderly succession underscores the importance of leadership foresight. Effective leaders prioritize succession planning, ensuring seamless transitions.

If bees can, can't we?

✓ **Stay healthy.**

The queen bee prioritizes the hive's cleanliness and health, as it directly impacts egg-laying and colony continuity. Worker bees diligently maintain hive hygiene to ensure the queen's optimal conditions for egg-laying. Likewise, specialized bees regulate temperature and moisture levels, actively maintaining hive conditions.

Similarly, in our lives, prioritizing health alongside work is essential. Just as bees nurture their hive, we must nurture ourselves to maintain physical and mental well-being.

In today's stressful work environment, we often hear young people passing away due to heart disease, the food habits and pollution adds to the work environment and leads to this situation. It is important to take care of health in parallel to money.

If bees can, can't we?

✓ **Growth is inevitable.**

In the brief lifespan of a worker bee, it transitions through various roles, from housekeeping to nursing, repair work, hive guarding, and foraging. Remarkably, there are no formal progressions or increment letters, yet they seamlessly advance along their career paths, continuously upskilling themselves for the next level.

Similarly, in our careers, continual upskilling is essential for advancement. Just as worker bees adapt and evolve, we must strive to enhance our skills to progress.

If bees can, can't we?

✓ **Let's take a break.**

Bees exemplify unwavering commitment to their community's well-being. If a bee falls ill, it will voluntarily leave the hive, sacrificing its life or isolating itself to protect the rest. Working tirelessly, bees operate round the clock, 365 days a year, akin to nature's constants like the sun and moon.

In contrast, humans enjoy weekends, holidays, annual, sick, parental and various other leaves. With these provisions, can't we take necessary breaks while maintaining our commitment to work?

If bees can, can't we?

✓ **Focus.**

Bees demonstrate remarkable focus and discipline in their daily routine. As soon as the sun rises, they embark on their mission to gather food, diligently visiting flowers and returning to the hive before sunset. With no contracts, policies, or incentives, they simply execute their tasks with unwavering dedication. Whether foraging for nectar or maintaining hive cleanliness, bees remain steadfast in their objectives without deviation or distraction.

Likewise, we can learn from their focused approach and strive towards our own goals with determination and clarity.

If bees can, can't we?

## Conclusion

We see hangings outside houses "Home Sweet Home", but the home of bees holds this literal truth, as their hive is truly a sweet haven. While we're accustomed to thanking God for giving our daily bread, we must also express gratitude to these tiny creatures, without whom our tables would be barren. Humans are adaptable, they will find ways to survive if there are no bees, but until today, bees have tirelessly served our needs. Let's show appreciation by nurturing a flower plant at home, so that some bee will visit it to take some nectar out of it, a small gesture to honor these remarkable contributors to our well-being.

My sincere thanks to my friend Charles for taking me through the journey of learning about the bees.

"Hearing the buzzing sound of the bee,
I am reminded to,

Bee Happy

Bee Kind

Bee Thankful

Bee Grateful

Bee Positive

Bee Cool

Bee Nice.

So, let´s be the bee."

BE

*- BEE Happy Always –*

# The Pandemonium Of The Pandas

*"To be happy is more important than to be successful"* - BE

P andas captivate the hearts and minds of people in a way that only few other species in this earth can, they are a bundle of joy to watch. My knowledge of how a panda would look was purely based on the animated film "kung foo panda", the dragon warrior, nothing more. My first encounter with these lovable creatures was at the Edinburgh Zoo, the moment I came to know that pandas were part of the zoo, my interest increased, and that very moment I visited zoo.

The normal way to visit a zoo is in groups, friends or family, but I have always preferred to visit the zoo in solo, so that I decide where to spend more time. while I strolled through the zoo, there were signs directing towards the Pandas, excitement increased with every step. It was a dream come true moment for me, I was getting closer to seeing the animated character in reality.

Upon reaching their enclosure, the first look of the Panda was captivating, the two pandas were naughty to the core, one was always behind the other, bugging it and I slowly moved a little away to take a look at their enclosure and there was one more, he was happily munching the bamboos, lying on a rock. Lost in the moment, time seemed to slip away unnoticed, with an hour passing in what felt like mere minutes and I was in the same place for more than an hour.

I fell in love with the black and white giants at the zoo and immediately asked if I could volunteer on weekends. I was willing to do any work just to be near them. The zoo directed me to Barbara, a friendly woman who was excited to hear I was an animal lover. However, she stressed the importance of commitment since they rely heavily on volunteers. I assured her that my weekdays were occupied with work, but I was free on weekends and would be fully committed. She invited me to start that Sunday, marking the beginning of my journey as a proud zoo volunteer.

My work hours were from 8:00 AM to 3:00 PM, with a coffee break and lunch break. Coffee was free, but we had to bring our own lunch. I was thrilled to start, imagining I could choose the animals I'd work with. However, the reality was different, I was assigned wherever needed and didn't get to choose which animals to work with.

I was paired with another volunteer named Krishna, or Krish. I expected to feed and care for the animals, give presentations, and guide zoo tours. Instead, I ended up doing cleaning and occasionally helping lost visitors find their way. Volunteers didn't directly care for or feed the animals; that was handled by a trained team.

Still, I was happy to be close to the animals and visit the zoo for free. Over time, I felt a connection with the animals, I was reminded of my days in the TVS factory, the start of the day was to clean a machine assigned to me, I initially disliked it, but eventually, it felt like part of me. The same happened here with the animals.

It was a nice feel to see the people forgetting themselves looking at the animals and the pandas were the prime attraction for the visitors, you would always see a big crowd around them that you would have to peep at times to get a glimpse of them, unlike other animals. Next to the pandas were the elephants, but due to their height and

129

size, you don't need to really stretch yourself to see them, they were visible from anywhere around.

I began to look forward to the weekends, not for a break, but for my trip to the zoo, Krish was an animal freak, having worked in the zoo for long. His awareness about the animal kingdom was much larger, we used to talk, rather I listen to him while we work together. These visits to the zoo made me rethink my opinion on the captivity of animals, it's a safe place for them, they get their meal on time, the vet visits them regularly for their health checkups, there is no risk of any predator attacks, as they are secluded. Also a question would arise in my mind, if safety and regular meals is worth losing your freedom. It's like asking if life in prison is better because you're fed and sheltered, it's a tough question with no easy answer.

During our cleaning routine, Krish used to tell me a lot of interesting stories about the zoo and the animals living there.

## Can something roaming in this world be undiscovered?

Can something so remarkable roam the Earth unnoticed? I told Krish that pandas were my favorite animal at the zoo, and he asked if I knew how long they've existed. Surprisingly, pandas have been around for about 8 million years and they have appeared in ancient Chinese literature, yet they were only officially documented in 1869. It's astonishing that humanity, with all its exploration, missed these black-and-white wonders for so long. Since their discovery, pandas have captured hearts worldwide, leading to what's known as "pandamania." In

1961, the World Wide Fund for Nature (WWF) chose the panda as its official mascot. Pandas are native to China's Sichuan province, where bamboo forests provide their primary food source.

## Ambassadors of Peace in black and white

Krish shared that he was present when the pandas arrived at the zoo, drawing massive crowds. Hosting pandas isn't just about having a star attraction, it's tied to diplomatic agreements with China. These animals symbolize international connections, and any panda cubs born abroad are subject to strict agreements, either they have to be returned back to China or they will stay back for a heft cost. "Panda diplomacy" highlights the importance of these gentle giants as ambassadors of goodwill between nations. Zoos outside China host pandas, now rented rather than gifted by the Chinese government.

Our fascination with pandas goes beyond their cuteness; their appearance triggers the release of oxytocin, the "love hormone," making us feel affectionate and protective towards them. Pandas have a knack for making laziness look utterly adorable, their bamboo-eating lifestyle will make you fall in love with them. They've become icons of relaxation, even as love and mating often take a backseat to their leisurely lifestyle.

## The lion within the panda.

Pandas may not roar like a lion, but they certainly command respect with their formidable bite strength. Pandas possess incredibly powerful jaws capable of delivering a bite force comparable to that of a lion. This remarkable strength is essential for their diet, which primarily consists of tough bamboo stalks, with specialized jaw muscles and robust teeth, pandas are equipped to efficiently crush and digest bamboo.

## Love is (un)common.

China has a one child policy, but pandas are Masters of the 'No Child' Policy. Love and reproduction are universal, but pandas disinterest in mating poses a threat to their species continuity, compounded by habitat loss. Conservationists work to address this, emphasizing captive breeding and habitat preservation to ensure the survival of these iconic animals. some zoos in China have tried to play panda porn for these animals for hours together, to create interest and they believe that it worked.

My routine was to work until 3.00 in the evening and then take a walk around the zoo, assisting the visitors, telling some of the interesting stories that I know about the animals to the children, which made me realize that there was a storyteller within me. Not sure if the storyteller was existing and was exposed then or if he was born only then. In any case, there was a storyteller then onward.

I slowly built an habit of making it not only interesting but to instigate some value additions to life's lessons. I ask a question – what they feel like when they see the pandas and their obvious reply was "they are lovely", "they are cute" and so on. Then I ask them to watch them for a minute, keeping both their hands at the side of their eyes so that they see only the panda and nothing else, then to close their eyes and replay in their mind what they did and I ask them what did they learn from their action and the answers were different.

You can see the panda munching bamboos most of the time, if not sleeping, if not both of these, they will be playing happily. You can never see the panda serious, they are happy all the time. You can also try to play videos of the pandas, watch them for a minute, then close your eyes and think of their behavior, there will be lot of lessons to learn.

Life´s lessons I had learnt from the closed eyes of kids.

### Lesson #1: "Prioritizing Happiness Over Success"

One of the child said, "They know nothing but to eat and be just happy."

This simple statement about pandas carried a deep lesson. The word "just" before "happy" resonated, highlighting that being happy is more important than being successful. Pandas embody this philosophy, they eat, sleep, and play, spreading joy wherever they go. Watching them, even as they sleep, brings a sense of peace, they will be eating and holding the bamboo, they will go to sleep. Their behavior teaches us that prioritizing happiness over traditional achievements leads to a more fulfilling life. While it's good to pursue success, it shouldn't come at the cost of happiness.

### Lesson # 2 – Captain Cool.

Another child said, "they are just cool".

Yes, they are the apt examples of Captain Cool, they will be least concerned about the crowd around, they won´t even take a look at you, but they will be busy all the time eating and sleeping. Can you call it busy to sleep and eat? Yes, pandas are those busy cool guys all the time eating and sleeping.

**Lesson # 3 – Be lovable.**

"They are just lovable, that's it"

How can you like someone who does nothing but just sleep and eat? Yes, with the pandas, you will not just like but love them for what their behavior of just to sleep and eat. Let the panda's charm inspire you to spread love and warmth, making the world a more lovable place, one cuddle at a time.

**Lesson # 4 – Live and let live.**

I was explaining to a kid that in China, these pandas are their national treasure, that they have allocated a huge bamboo forest for the pandas, for their wellbeing, to ensure that this species of bears in black and white survives. We all know the popular James Bond 007 movie "Live and Let Die", the moto of the pandas is "Live and Let Live", yes with this huge bamboo forest, not only do the pandas live but numerous other species as well get to live.

**Lesson # 5 – Do only what you are to do.**

*"Work while you work, Play while you play.*

*One thing each time, that is the way. All that you do, do with your might."*

If the pandas are eating, sleeping or playing – they do just that, only that, nothing else, no distractions. We normally watch television or mobile while eating, so you do not really enjoy the food nor the show in the television. We often see dinner get togethers with friends or family, where most will be on their mobile.

## Lesson # 6 – The power of power nap.

I have heard that in Japan, people take a power nap during the day and resume work, which helps to do work fresh and better. I had watched these pandas take a power nap between their busy munching routine, it will be so adoring to see it eating and suddenly his eyes will close and his head will be tilted sleeping for a few minutes and the bamboo stays in its hand, suddenly he will remember that he has a lot of work (to eat) to do, he wakes up and resumes eating the bamboo in hand.

With the covid pandemic, started the routine of work from home and I realized the power of the power nap, a 15 minute nap and its like a fresh new day starting when you resume. Give it a try, continue if it helps.

## The kung foo panda

"Kung Fu Panda" is a 2008 animated film set in Ancient China's Valley of Peace. Po, a lovable giant panda, unexpectedly becomes the chosen Dragon Warrior, tasked with mastering kung fu to defend against the formidable Tai Lung. Initially doubting his abilities, Po finds inspiration and courage to confront Tai Lung, proving that even the most unlikely heroes can rise to greatness through determination and belief in themselves.

**What I loved the most in the movie.**

The movie on the whole has a lot of positivity, still everyone will have their own liking, in which way, what I liked most was the power of belief and confidence in one's abilities to achieve success will be highlighted by Po's dad's wisdom, Po asks his dad on how come the soup is always extraordinarily delicious every time though made of the same ingredients and the reply comes, it is the belief that it will come out special that makes it truly special. It's a valuable lesson that resonates beyond the kitchen, reminding us of the transformative power of positive thinking in all aspects of life. It is the belief that is more important.

**The lessons from the (panda) movie.**

**Lesson # 1: "Embrace the Unfamiliar"**

Master Shifu's advice to Po echoes the importance of stepping outside one's comfort zone. Despite initial reluctance and failure, Po learns that growth and success lie beyond familiarity. His journey teaches us the value of perseverance, even in the face of setbacks, inspiring us to embrace challenges and keep striving for greatness.

**Lesson #2: "Embracing Identity and Versatility in Leadership"**

Po's inner conflict reflects a key question leaders face: "Who am I?" Leaders must adapt, embracing different roles, coach, manager, or cheerleader, depending on the situation. Like Po, who is both a warrior and a teacher, leaders need versatility. Effective leadership involves self- awareness, clear goals, building and guiding the right team, and navigating challenges.

Ultimately, leadership is a blend of roles and experiences, with the leader's unique self as the driving force behind success.

### Lesson #3: "Empowering Individual Excellence"

Po's leadership journey involves empowering others by recognizing and nurturing their unique strengths. Instead of making others like him, he helps them reach their full potential. True leadership is about celebrating individuality, unlocking collective potential, and guiding each team member to become their best self.

### Lesson #4: "The Power of Collective Strength"

Po's leadership shows sacrifice and unity, risking himself for his team's safety while relying on their collective strength to succeed. Effective leaders do the same, prioritizing the team's welfare and fostering trust. By empowering others, leaders unlock collective potential, helping teams overcome challenges and grow stronger together.

### Lesson #5: "The Power Lies Within You"

In the world of Kung Fu Panda, the ultimate lesson is that there's no secret ingredient to being a great leader; it's all about you. Every leader possesses the potential for greatness, it's a matter of self-belief and unwavering confidence, even in the face of doubt from others. Like Po discovering his inner strength, effective leaders embrace their unique qualities and lead with authenticity, knowing that the power to inspire and achieve lies within themselves.

## Lesson #6: "Tailoring Motivation to Individuality"

In Kung Fu Panda, leadership means recognizing that everyone thrives differently. Po's love for food was his motivation. Effective leaders understand and embrace these differences, tailoring motivation to each person's strengths and interests. By doing so, they unlock individual potential and foster collective success.

## The great lesson

The pandas just do what they like, just eat, sleep and play and they are taken care so well by everyone around, they are so much loved for what they do and they just do what they like the most. I have heard the Indian film artist Kamal Hassan say many a times that he is on a holiday always doing what he likes and he is paid for it. So can you, find what you like and see if you can get an income out of it, then you do not have to work, not even for a day in a year, but just do what you like and you earn your living.

If pandas can, can't we?

## The end of the journey.

It became more a pilgrimage than a visit to the zoo, the very purpose of a pilgrimage is to understand life's lessons better, my journey to the zoo came to an end very soon, it was hardly 4 months and my project was shifted to Southampton, which is very normal in a software company, to be shifted from one project or place to another.

I bid good bye to my volunteer friends, the zoo and most of all, my dear animal friends, I walked across the zoo one last time, to bid adieu to my loving friends. Pandas being the first, the second best thing I liked in the zoo was the penguin walk and penguin feeding, it was a treat to the eyes to watch them walking and it ends with the penguins being fed with fishes. The penguin parade in the Philip Island in Australia is more a natural one with hundreds of penguin parading together, but this is a different experience.

I walked out of the zoo with a heavy heart, it was a difficult moment. Every week when I walk out of the zoo I knew I would return the subsequent weekend, but this time I knew that this would be my last. The journey was short but the learnings were big.

The primary and ultimate lesson from pandas is just being a panda is happiness. To prioritize joy and fulfillment above all else. Ultimately, the greatest lesson from pandas is that happiness is not just a destination but a journey, to be cherished and embraced every step of the way.

*"To be happy is more important than to be successful"*
**BE**

*- Be Happy Always –*

**- be a panda -**

♣

# The Tale of Whales

**"Everything whale be okay." - BE**

I moved from Edinburgh to Eastleigh, near Southampton. Despite a zoo being in southampton, I never visited since they had no pandas. A month later, my friend Krish called, joking that the zoo animals missed me. In truth, I missed them. He asked me if I would be interested in joining on a sailing experience, he had a friend who owns a yacht in Southampton. The plan was to sail around the Isle of Wight with an overnight stay at Bembridge. I was thrilled and quickly asked when we would leave.

On Saturday morning, Krish and two other volunteer friends joined me, we took a train to Southampton and went straight to meet Paul, who would take us on a two-day sailing trip, he was a very friendly person. We walked from the train station to a place near the harbor where lot of yacht were docked, in one of the yacht, it was written "The Greens" in green color, Paul asked us to board the yacht, said that we would be spending the next 2 days in this beautiful yacht, he said the name "The Greens" was his family name. I expected the yacht to be small, but it was surprisingly big, comfortably fitting all five of us. As we set sail, the yacht rocked with the tides, which was a little scary at first. We had life jackets for each of us, Krish assured me not to worry since Paul had been sailing with his family since he was a child, so we were in safe hands.

As we sailed, I saw land on both sides since Southampton port is set a bit inland, almost like backwaters. But soon, we moved into the open sea, losing sight of land with water all around us. The waves calmed, and Paul mentioned that the sea's changing nature is what makes the journey exciting. He also shared that he has sailed in different parts of the world, said we might spot dolphins if we're lucky, which sparked our curiosity.

Inside the yacht, there was ample space with sofas all around and a toilet at the rear. It was cozy and comfortable, perfect for relaxing. This was my first time venturing into the sea, and I was excited. Paul turned off the motor, and we stopped in the middle of the water. He served us hot coffee, which felt refreshing as we sat surrounded by the sea. Paul shared his experience of sailing in Norway for whale watching. He recalled encountering whales much larger than the yacht, yet gentle and friendly. He explained that a skilled guide knows how to sail without disturbing the whales, turning off the engine at the right moments to earn the whale's trust.

Once they feel safe, they glide gracefully alongside the boat. Watching these majestic creatures exhale with a gentle spray, like a grand aquatic fountain, is a mesmerizing sight. My interest in going on a whale-watching trip grew even stronger.

Paul mentioned he had never seen elephants and wished to visit Africa to see them. I told him we have elephants in India too. Elephants on land and whales in the ocean are both gentle giants in their environments. Despite their different habitats, they share similarities and play crucial roles in maintaining the balance of their ecosystems. Dolphins, like miniature whales, are incredibly friendly, especially towards humans. Like the panda being my favorite, Paul's favorite was the whale, he had a wealth of information about not only sailing, but about whales too.

## Whale Myths.

While near the Isle of Wight, Paul let me steer the yacht, saying everyone would get a turn when the tides were calm. It reminded me of the first time I rode a bicycle or drove a car, an unexpected and thrilling experience. Steering felt easy when the water was calm, and I could even manage it with one hand, unlike driving, since there was no traffic to worry about.

There was an antique-looking binocular on board, labeled "The Greens," reflecting the family's long history of sailing. As I looked through it, I noticed something gray popping up and diving near the coast. To my surprise, it was a pod of dolphins! I tried steering closer, but Paul advised against it, explaining that the motor's noise might scare them away. He turned off the engine, and we were surrounded by the peaceful sounds of waves and birds. Using the binoculars, we watched the dolphins glide effortlessly through the water. Even Paul, an experienced sailor, was excited, showing that the sight of dolphins is magical for everyone, not just first-timers. Each time they dove back into the sea, it made me marvel at the beauty hidden beneath the ocean's surface.

We moved on, and Paul shared some myths he heard while sailing in the West. In Hinduism, a visiting crow is seen as an ancestor, and a similar belief exists in the Pacific, where people call dolphins to the shore, believing them to be their ancestors. Some dolphins do come and play around for some time. In the Amazon, dolphins are thought to change genders and, like mermaids, lure people into the water to harm them. Paul also mentioned Pakicetus, which lived 50 million years ago in what is now Pakistan. It's considered the first whale, with the body of a land animal and the head of a whale.

## Can you believe that whales were land animals before?

It's amazing to know that whales once lived on land. About 50 million years ago, they transitioned to the ocean, though they are still mammals, not fish. Whales share an ancient ancestor with humans from 90 million years ago. They show strong parental care, nursing their young for up to 18 months before teaching them to be independent, similar to humans. Living in pods, they work together to hunt and migrate, passing down knowledge through generations.

## Conscious breathing.

Humans breathe involuntarily, a constant rhythm ensuring our survival. Conversely, whales are conscious breathers, controlling when to inhale. While humans use only a fraction of their brain's potential, cetaceans exhibit exceptional cerebral abilities. During sleep, they employ a unique strategy, shutting down one brain hemisphere to rest while the other remains vigilant, ensuring uninterrupted breathing. Unlike land animals, cetaceans can't simply sleep submerged; they must surface for air. By alternating brain activity, they achieve restful sleep in open waters, navigating the challenges of their marine habitat with remarkable adaptability.

## Cultural tradition in Laguna.

In the southern coastal region of Brazil, an extraordinary partnership between dolphins and humans has flourished for 140 years, a cultural tradition passed down through generations. As wild bottlenose dolphins grace the lagoon, local fishers keenly observe their behavior, casting nets at strategic moments to enhance their fish harvest. A 15-year study by the Max Planck

Institute, using drones and underwater imaging, highlighted the mutual benefits of this practice. However, the tradition is at risk due to declining mullet populations and less interest from younger generations. The findings, published in the Proceedings of the National Academy of Sciences, reveal the challenge of preserving cultural practices while addressing environmental issues. I always carry a notebook and pen to jot down interesting information, which I later review to learn more about the topic.

## About Tahlequah.

Whales, like elephants and certain other species, exhibit a matriarchal society. Led by their mothers or grandmothers, they dwell in pods, where essential life values and survival skills are imparted from one generation to the next. This familial structure fosters respect for elders and a deep bond among members. In a poignant display of maternal devotion, Tahlequah, an orca in the northeastern Pacific, captured global attention in 2018 when she carried her stillborn calf for 17 days across thousands of miles, refusing to let it sink. This act of grieving resonated with people worldwide, evoking parallels to human emotions. Even as the calf's body decomposed and became burdensome, Tahlequah's podmates aided her, reflecting a communal support system similar to human families. Notably, one of Tahlequah's adopters was Malia Obama, daughter of former US President Barack Obama.

Listening to Paul made the time fly, and soon it was lunchtime. Eating on the yacht was a unique experience, and Paul was careful not to litter, reflecting his family's long sailing tradition. We saw dolphins again and noticed the white rocks of the Needles, three chalk stacks at the island's western tip. By evening, I took a short nap below deck and woke up to tea. We arrived in Bembridge around 7 PM, finding it charmingly different from city life. After docking, we explored the town, the feel and look of an island has always been different from that of a normal city in a land, we had dinner at a local restaurant, and then went to a campsite for the night.

We setup our tents, continued our talking, Paul was giving more insights about his whale watching experience, he said that it totally depends on the experience of the guide, he can make it look like a conversation between the yacht and the animal. He was very concerned about whaling and whale fall.

### What is a whale fall?

When a whale dies, it's termed a whale fall, sinking to the ocean floor and providing vital nutrients for deep-sea life. However, whaling persists in countries like Japan, Iceland, and Norway, where it's legal. Thousands of whales are killed annually, each fetching a huge amount.

**Poop worthy.**

Paul was telling about the story of the poop and I was happy to share the story about the poop of the elephants, it was more of an exchange of information. Across the globe, the air we breathe is enriched by the oceans, where whales play a crucial role. These majestic creatures embark on epic journeys, diving deep to feed and resurfacing to breathe, leaving behind a trail of nutrient-rich excrement. This whale poop serves as fertilizer for phytoplankton, tiny oceanic plants that not only sustain marine life but also combat climate change by absorbing carbon dioxide and producing oxygen. Remarkably, phytoplankton generate up to 85% of the oxygen in our atmosphere, illustrating the profound interconnectedness between oceans and terrestrial ecosystems. Furthermore, when phytoplankton perish, they transfer billions of metric tons of carbon from the atmosphere to the ocean floor, mitigating environmental impacts. Thus, the abundance of whale poop fuels a cycle of life in the oceans, supporting diverse marine ecosystems and ultimately benefiting all living beings on this earth, underscoring the vital importance of preserving these magnificent creatures and their habitats.

**Whale vomit.**

Paul added that not just the poop, but even the whale vomit is of value, otherwise called ambergris, is prized in perfumery for its unique scent-enhancing properties. Despite its name, ambergris is a secretion, not vomit, produced by whales. Its rarity and fragrance make it a valuable ingredient in perfumes, showcasing the intriguing relationship between whales and the fragrance industry.

## The Whale industry - There is no value if it doesn't come with a price tag.

Paul was very concerned that we talk about whaling and that it is injustice, but we cannot do much rather than sympathize, I was reminded of the words I once read, "do not sympathize, it´s of no use", rather attempt to help. Paul went on to showcase the industry that the whales were running. I was going through related topics, came across an analysis by Ralph Chami, a financial economist, working with the International Monetary Fund (IMF) and I was astonished looking at the figures.

Whales play a crucial role in our ecosystem, with their value estimated at around $3 million per whale by Ralph Chami of the IMF. This value comes from their ability to absorb $CO_2$ and produce oxygen. Despite their importance, we often overlook this because their benefits are free, much like the air we breathe.

A single whale can capture as much $CO_2$ as 1,500 trees and plays a key role in the planet's health. They capture about 37 billion tons of $CO_2$ each year. When whales die, they sink to the ocean floor, taking about 33 tons of $CO_2$ with them and removing it from the atmosphere for centuries.

Phytoplankton, which absorb around 37 billion tons of $CO_2$ annually, are crucial for this process. Krill, which whales eat, feed on phytoplankton. Whale waste fertilizes these plankton, enhancing their carbon absorption through a process called the "whale pump."

On land, elephants have a similar impact. Each forest elephant is valued at $2.6 million for their role in forest health and regeneration. They help with carbon storage by consuming vegetation and dispersing seeds.

Seagrass is even more valuable, estimated at $2.3 trillion. Like whales and elephants, seagrass performs essential functions, making these natural systems invaluable despite their free provision of services.

Whale watching alone constitutes a billion-dollar tourism industry, generating around $2.1 billion annually. It's time we stop their exploitation and start appreciating the invaluable services they provide. It's time to tap into our latent sixth sense before it's too late.

Some people make the beautiful by just living in it, whales in the ocean and elephants in the land are prime examples of this, they just eat – move – sleep – excrete, nothing more, but their value add is immeasurable. A living whale holds immeasurable value, yet once deceased, it tragically becomes known as floating gold. Economists and financial analysts serve as translators, converting these ecological services into monetary terms, as human comprehension often necessitates financial quantification. Sadly, anything offered free of charge tends to be undervalued, but the true cost of losing these majestic creatures is far greater than any currency could measure.

**The sad story.**

The tragic reality is that while there are no documented cases of whales harming humans, thousands of these magnificent creatures are killed annually. Whaling persists in countries like Iceland, Japan, and Norway, posing a grave threat to whale populations worldwide. Humanity has not understood yet that the returns are much higher if they are alive.

**The Whale Lessons.**

My thought of looking at Paul as just a sailor was wrong, he said that there are tons of lessons to learn from the whales just like their weight, we ought to see what we can learn from this tons of weight, not chop them into pieces and just eat. My take away's from Paul's tent sessions at Bembridge.

**Find the leader in you - be the leader in you.**

Just as a lion reigns in the jungle and an eagle soars in the skies, the whale commands the oceans. Just like the lions have their own hunting strategy, Orcas otherwise called as killer whales have theirs too, to hunt in groups. The target is to get the prey, does not matter how they achieve it, whether it is solo or in groups.

So, should be the leader, to have the target in mind, ensure its achieved at any cost, it may be a solo performance or a team work, but achieving the goal is prime. This is not just for the leader at the top, it is for every role that you play, to be the leader in it, you may be a project manager, a developer or an administrator, each task demands dedication and mastery, ensuring that in every endeavor, one leads with proficiency and diligence. From managing projects to sweeping streets, leadership lies in the commitment to excellence and the pursuit of mastery in every role.

If a whale can, can't we?

### *"Be the leader in whatever you do."*

✓ **Be Innovative.**

The orcas teach the younger ones on the techniques of hunting, on how to hunt a puppy seal which is in the shore, in shallow waters, orcas with their body movements near the shore, create a sort of wave that would suck the puppy seal to the sea and become a prey, this act is quite dangerous for the orcas, where it could cost its life itself, as its difficult to breath for the orcas in shallow waters near the shore, but with experience it does it and they teach these techniques to their younger ones.

Similarly, we can improve by embracing innovation and staying open to new ideas. Just as orcas are innovative and learn from the experts in their group, we can also gain valuable insights from those around us to enhance our skills and become leaders through continuous improvement and innovation.

If a whale can, can't we?

### *"Innovate, Craft, Succeed."*

### ✓ Be an effective communicator.

Whales are renowned for their sophisticated communication abilities, spanning vast distances across oceans and persisting for hours, Sperm whales hold the title of the ocean's loudest creatures. Similarly, human evolution has granted us the capability to communicate globally through advanced technologies like satellite communication. Yet, despite these advancements, mastering the art of communication remains elusive. Many corporations prioritize communication and soft skills training for employees, recognizing the complexity of effective communication. While humans possess innate communication abilities, true effectiveness requires refinement through experience or training.

*"The most important thing in communication is hearing what isn't said." - Peter Drucker*

### ✓ Be Empathetic.

In different habitats, killer whales, or orcas, actively pursue lion seals, creatures capable of holding their breath underwater for as long as 30 minutes. Orcas possess remarkable abilities, they can detect seals within a 1 km radius and reach speeds of up to 55 km/h while swimming.

Yet, they must maintain constant vigilance during the hunt. Lion seals, on the other hand, have evolved a biomechanical alarm system sensitive to orca communication, compelling the orcas into silence until they are within striking distance of their prey.

Despite their best efforts, young orcas sometimes make sounds that alert the seals, resulting in failed hunts. Orcas are physiologically adapted for deep dives, but the lion seals' superior breath-holding capabilities force orcas to surface for air, adding complexity to the hunt.

Mistakes during these endeavors can be costly, depleting the group's energy reserves by over a million calories. However, in a remarkable display of social cohesion, orcas forgive the errors of their junior members, prioritizing teamwork over punishment.

*"To err is human, to forgive is divine."*

✓ **Be a good team player, teamwork is smart work.**

Orcas possess remarkable echolocation abilities, allowing them to locate seals within a range of 1 kilometer. When hunting in frozen seas, they target seals resting on ice floes. Although unable to reach the seals directly on the ice, orcas employ a strategic approach to dislodging them from their safe perch.

Orcas demonstrate an understanding that breaking the ice floe is necessary to access the seal. Employing a specialized hunting strategy, they swim in synchronized formations at speeds of up to 30 kilometers per hour. Together, they create a unique wave and water vortex, effectively shattering the ice floe into smaller pieces. The force of the wave propels the seal into the water.

Remarkably, orcas also recognize that the presence of smaller ice fragments could aid the seal in hiding or escaping. Consequently, they systematically clear the surrounding area of broken ice, ensuring the seal has no refuge. This coordinated and team-oriented behavior underscores the intelligence and adaptability of these magnificent creatures.

Think of it like a war strategy: the cavalry strikes first, then the elephants break through fort gates, in what angles are the forces supposed to attack, every single move has to be meticulously planned by the king and the forces, it is a teamwork, coordination was crucial. If orcas can achieve such teamwork in nature, can't we?

Only when you work as a team, can you achieve greater heights, keep aside your ego and work towards the organization goals.

*"Swimming together,*
*hunting together for sustenance."*

✓ **Family values.**

The Whale's Wisdom: Whales, notably sperm whales, epitomize the importance of family and community. Living in tightly knit pods spanning generations, they exhibit profound affection and care for one another, reflecting the deep bonds within their social structures. This highlights the invaluable role of nurturing and supporting familial and communal ties. Humpback whales undertake extensive migrations, traveling thousands of miles from polar regions to warmer waters for mating and to avoid harsh weather, this great migration has been passed on over generations and being followed meticulously.

*"Let's live the whale way."*

✓ **The end of the journey.**

We slept late in the night after the tent session, my notepad was full of information. We left Bembridge the next day, did a full circle of the island and reached Southampton around 3.00 in the evening. We bid goodbye to Paul, thanked him not only for the sailing experience but for the valuable lessons. I asked Krish on when do we plan for the whale watching experience and his reply was soon.

If whale´s can, can´t we?

**- follow the whale for w(hale) elthiness –**

*- Be Happy Always –*

♦

# *What Next?*

**"Shaping Dreams, Sculpting Success" - BE**

Now that we have walked through the forest, visiting various gurus, it is apparent that a guru is not someone in a saffron robe sitting under a tree, but rather they pervade everywhere. This idea comes close to the saying that God is omnipresent; His teachings are everywhere, and it is for us to tune ourselves to the right frequency, to listen, just like the radio. Listening isn't enough; you need to dream big. Dreaming big isn't enough either; you need to plan. Planning alone isn't enough; you need to act. Start your planning and action today, at this very moment. Don't postpone it to tomorrow; start living today. Sculpt your life with your wishes. Dream big for a better tomorrow. If tomorrow isn't better, believe that the day after will be, there may be a delay, never a denial. Remember, it is more important to be happy than to be successful in life. It is the journey that is more beautiful than the destination itself. Life is a journey, so sit back, relax, and enjoy it. Don't be in a hurry; you are not on a racetrack. Your friends may overtake you, but it doesn't matter. Try recalling a drive from home to the office; you may have someone overtake you, only to see them waiting at the next traffic signal, most of the time. Remember that you are going at your speed to reach your destination, which is your office; you just need to be on time. Others in the road, are going at a different speed to reach a different destination and purpose. Both are different. Continue your journey at your own pace. Live life your way.

If an animal can, can't we? Shouldn't we? Let's start the planning today.

## Let's start the planning today.

### Identify your favorite.

Now that we have seen what we can learn from the gentle giants of the land, air and the seas, let's identify your favorite, put a tick.

| | |
|---|---|
| The Gentle giants – the elephant | ☐ |
| The V (We) secret of birds | ☐ |
| Be(e)aware of the bees | ☐ |
| The pandemonium of the pandas | ☐ |
| The tale of whales | ☐ |

### The Why?

Why did you put a tick against the animal, what characteristics of the animal fascinated you the most.

### The What Next?

If this is my favorite animal and if this is the reason I fell in love with it, what am I going to change about myself starting from today, not just today, but right now. You may wonder how simply listing "The What" will work, right? Have no doubts; it's the mind that decides everything - it's you who decides.

Take a nice clean sheet of paper (if possible, made from elephant poop!) ☺ - Write down in your own handwriting; don't print. There's a difference when you write - your heart and mind will be listening to what your hand writes. Don't worry if your handwriting is bad; it's for you to understand, not for someone else to read and correct like an answer sheet. Preferable use multi and bright colors, watching this colorful paper daily, you will notice your life becoming colorful too.

If your favorite animal is the adorable Panda, then go on. It's challenging to match all their characteristics, so select a few.

| The characteristics | The Lesson | The Tick | The Change | Review Date |
|---|---|---|---|---|
| Be the Panda | | | | |
| The Happiness Index | To Prioritizing Happiness Over Success | ✓ | I will count the number of happy times - good moments I had for the day before I go to sleep | 1 Month from now |
| The Attitude | To be the Captain Cool | ✓ | I will work towards solution, not worry about the problem. Will think of what next - not think about what happened. | 1 Month from now |
| The way of living | Be lovable | ✓ | I will work to ensure I am loved by everyone around - | 1 Month from now |
| The value add | Live and let live | | | |
| The discipline | Do only what you are to do | | | |
| The work style | The power of power nap | | | |

If you favorite is a different animal, pick the lessons they had to offer, you can also pick and choose from different animals - stick this on a thick piece of cardboard. Read it twice a day: first thing in the morning, even before you brush your teeth, and before you go to sleep. Spend a few minutes standing in front of it, reading it. Even if you think you know what's written, read it again. Reflect on whether you've done what you wrote. If not, don't worry; there's always tomorrow. It's true that you need to live for today, but if you haven't, start living from tomorrow onwards. Tomorrow will be your today again.

Add another sheet with the date, day and number of feel-good moments. If you familiar with MS Excel, put it in an excel sheet – update it daily – put a graph at end of month – see the trend – it will give you clues on what gives you more happness – so that, you can do more of it. You may notice more feel-good moments on specific days. Reflect on what you did on those days and repeat it. It could be a visit to a temple or church or doing something kind for someone or it could be partying with friends.

| Date | Day | Count | Category | A Brief |
|------|-----|-------|----------|---------|
| | Fri | 4 | 1. Party | Get-together with old friends |
| | | | 2. Helping | Cooked dinner for friends |
| | | | 3. Goal | Helped a stranger in the public bus |
| | | | 4. Exercise | 1 Hour of walk |
| | | | 5. Passion | Music Lesson for 1 Hour |
| | Sat | 2 | 1. Health | 1.5 Hours of walk |
| | | | 2. Passion | Music Lesson for 1 Hour |

If you find that the routine to walk is one of your feel good moment, ensure to never miss it. You may feel that one hour of walking is a waste of time, but remember, life only comes once. You spend time with your team, friends, neighbors, and others, but this one hour of walking is time spent with the most beautiful person in the world: yourself. It's not idle time; you can multitask. Put on your headset, listen to your favorite music, or if you don't find music useful, listen to podcasts or something informative. Ideally, walk while listening to the person inside you; there is an interesting personality residing there inside.

Set a review date, perhaps a month later. If you've achieved few or even one of the goals you wrote down, it is a success. If you feel it's easier said than done, remember: the phrase we often read throughout this book, like - "if an ant can, can't you?". Sometimes, we need to draw inspiration from these simple and humble beings.

*"To read isn't enough, dream big!*

*To dream isn't enough, plan today!*

*To plan isn't enough, act now!*

*Not just now, but right now!"*

*- BE*

## What next for me?

*"Just when the caterpillar thought the world was over, it became a butterfly.*

*There is always something more."*

We pause here, but the journey and the learnings continue. My path alongside animals is a lifelong one, for I have fallen deeply in love with them. There is so much more to explore, many more animals to meet, and countless lessons to learn from the depths of the jungles.

In the work environment, especially in fields like Information Technology, appreciation can be scarce. Often, it feels like the mindset is, "I'm paying you, so just do your job," with little recognition for the effort put in. This isn't true of every project, but I've worked on some, where acknowledgment was nonexistent, leading to moments of frustration.

I had a friend Rishi while I worked in the UK, who was always cheerful, no matter what the circumstance was. One day, I asked him how he managed to stay so positive. His answer surprised me: he said it's because he liked donkeys. Curious, I asked why he chose donkeys over majestic animals like lions or elephants. What relevance did a donkey have to his happiness?

161

He asked me if I truly knew what a donkey's life was like. I responded with the usual stereotypes: stubborn, lazy, and not particularly bright. But he told me that's a misconception. Donkeys, he said, are the epitome of resilience. They bear heavy burdens without complaint, their faces showing no strain despite the weight they carry. From this, he learned how to remain content, no matter the difficulties around him. His words struck a chord with me, I headed to a donkey farm, which opened up a new world of understanding.

I will continue sharing my experiences with animals, which ended up not just as visits but as educational journeys. Each encounter has offered me wisdom and a deeper understanding of these amazing creatures. I've been fortunate to have unique experiences wherever I've gone, learning from animals and understanding them on a deeper level. Perhaps it's the principle of Buddhism: what you seek is what you find.

### *The unheard sound of the jungle bells.*

#### *"Only in silence can you truly hear the whispers" - BE*

My humble advice to the reader is this: to truly experience the unconditional love of an animal, consider adopting a pet. If you're not ready for that commitment, find ways to connect with animals at your own level. Visit a zoo or an animal farm, pick your favorite animal, sit close, and observe. In that moment, you'll begin to hear the unheard sounds of the jungle's bells. The roar of the lion or the trumpet of the elephant may be loud, but their lessons are whispered, to hear the whispers, you must quieten your mind and tune in deeply.

For me, this journey will continue into the jungle in search of other lovable and humble beings that inhabit it, for I have forever fallen in love with them. I am a lost wanderer in the woods.

*"There is something to learn from everything."*

*- BE*

*- Be Happy Always –*